# We're Thankful for the Moisture

ELI McCANN

# We're Thankful for the Moisture

A Gay Guy's Guide to Mormon Faith, Family, and Fruit Preservation

Eli McCann

Signature Books | 2026 | Salt Lake City

*For my husband, Skylar, who insists on buying physical copies of* The Salt Lake Tribune *so he can read my columns in absolute silence and without laughing once, before setting down the paper and saying, vaguely, "This one was special."*

 Published by Signature Books.

Signature Books is a registered trademark of Signature Books Publishing, LLC. Printed in the USA using paper from sustainably harvested sources.

Join our mail list at www.signaturebooks.com for details on events and related titles we think you'll enjoy.

Design by Jason Francis
Cover illustration by Pat Bagley

FIRST EDITION | 2026

LIBRARY OF CONGRESS CONTROL NUMBER: 2026930121

Paperback ISBN: 978-1-56085-532-3
Ebook ISBN: 978-1-56085-510-1

# Contents

# Preface

As a child I loved to write, enough so that my parents came to expect to hear at every parent-teacher conference that I had trouble paying attention in class and instead sat scribbling away in my notebook. I'd jot down funny stories I made up. These writings are some of my greatest treasures now—they are certainly funny, but not for the reasons I intended when I penned them.

By my mid-20s, I began blogging, and I never stopped. I think I might be the last blogger in America, continuing to write mostly humor stories on my website, itjustgetsstranger.com. Through the years, I've been able to share stories from my life with a growing audience across the world, with a dream of one day publishing a book of humor essays.

Then in 2022, Peggy Fletcher Stack, *Salt Lake Tribune* religion reporter and A-List Celebrity from my childhood, reached out to me for a complicated story related to my professional expertise, which she was in the throes of researching. Too intimidated to say no, I agreed to meet with her. Over lunch, after it became clear I was completely unhelpful to her, Peggy pivoted abruptly and asked if I'd be interested in writing a humor column for the paper.

Not one to turn down any invitation to get more attention, I enthusiastically agreed. Peggy then connected me with *Tribune* managing editor David Noyce, who has spent the past three years reviewing my columns and deleting all the profanity, which makes him the only person in the world who has the authority to force me to stop swearing. (Dave, my mother is jealous, but grateful.)

Since 2022, I have written, like, 40 columns? There might be more. Or there might be fewer. Unfortunately, there's no way to check. Unless you read this book.

Writing these columns has given me an opportunity to explore the culture from which I spawned—quirks, blemishes, beauty and all. It has also allowed for a critical mass of social media users whose names are some variation of PATRIOT6444235 to shout online such helpful feedback as "ELI CLEERLY HATES THE CHURCH END NEEDS 2 REPENTANCE!" and "HOW IS THIS NEWS."

Although readers have sometimes objected to what they perceive to be my criticism of or apologetics for The Church of Jesus Christ of Latter-day Saints and the culture that surrounds it (sometimes both accusations for the very same sentence!), I think I'm sincere in saying that neither has ever been my objective. It's been my view for a long time that surely the tithing I paid for nearly three decades purchased at least the right to poke fun at the Tabernacle Choir's muumuus.

When I began writing for *The Tribune,* Dave or Peggy, or both of them in unison like creepy twins who speak in chorus, encouraged me to strive to be playful but never mean-spirited. This has always felt like easy advice to follow as I've written the columns now published in this exceptional book (if I do say so myself). While I may now be a heathen who would fail a temple recommend interview faster than you can incorrectly pronounce "foyer," it has never been my impulse to mock my roots.

Mormonism and the culture it shapes are a part of who I am, for better or worse. It's a big part of why I had to go to therapy for a good chunk of my 30s. But it's also the reason I have an impulse to organize a casserole calendar when I find out a neighbor broke their leg. Or jar pickles to give away. You'll never convince me growing up in the church did not benefit me at all. But you'll also never convince me to return or raise my son in it. Unless, of course, Cher gets baptized and joins my ward choir.

There's something freeing about realizing you're not required to have a one-dimensional view of a complicated issue. For me, writing these columns has allowed me to process what I feel about being a gay married dad in Zion's headquarters of Salt Lake City. I could resent much of it and be grateful for the rest. Or even apathetic. But instead, I've found it's easier to find most of it funny. The cosplaying pioneers on July 24. The fact that I know every word to every song in *Saturday's Warrior*. The occasional encounter with a photo from my childhood where I'm dressed up as a tumbleweed for our ward's roadshow production of *Oh, South Jordan!*

Nearly all of it is hilarious.

And at the root of the amusement there is something deeply human about the quirks. When I think about my often silly childhood and the cheesy and earnest activities and sayings that narrated my youth, it occurs to me that so much of this was a result of well-meaning grownups who believed in something, trying to build community in the best way they knew how. And while I don't believe in many of the same things they believed in, I confess I'm profoundly grateful for much of what they did for me, even if it was sometimes deeply flawed.

So no, I don't think any of this is as simple as "church good" or "church bad." I don't even think the truth lies between those options. And perhaps that makes me a confused critic who is also somehow an apologist. But that's okay—at least I'm still laughing as I write about it.

The good people at Signature Books, whom I bullied into publishing all of this, read my columns as a collection and suggested that it reads like a memoir of my life in some ways. Because of that, we've elected to organize the entries roughly chronologically, with my childhood stories at the front and stories of marriage and new fatherhood rounding out the back end. You'll also find some marvelous cartoons—originally published with my columns—by the ever-talented, award-winning Pat Bagley, who has more than once coaxed me to go to his house for a potluck so he could feed me whiskey (my love language).

For the uninitiated, I have also included a Glossary at the back of this book, roughly defining common Latter-day Saint terms and jargon used throughout these stories. I wrote this Glossary while under the influence of a fever, so if any of it reads as incoherent to you, that's why.

Thank you for reading this nonsense and thank you for buying this book so I can blow all the money on bad cockfight bets.

XOXO, hugs and kisses

Eli McCann

P.S. This book is being published in loving memory of the Manti Pageant, may she rest in peace.

# We're Thankful for the Moisture

If you asked me to close my eyes and picture my most representative childhood memory, I'd see it immediately.

There I am, age 6, slouched over my mother's lap on a long bench, only half conscious, a clip-on bow tie digging into my neck. I'm staring at a green hymnbook, a foot in front of my face, poking out of a wooden box attached to the bench in front of us. A woman with a permed mullet I had last seen the week before when she scolded me and my friends for riding our bikes over her carefully manicured lawn has just stepped up to a podium at the front of the room. She folds her arms and closes her eyes. After a two-second pause, she breathes into the microphone in earnestness: "Our dear, kind, gracious Heavenly Father, we are thankful for the mois-chur that we have been receivun'."

Three decades later, I made the mistake of telling my husband about this phrase just after he moved to Utah and began to learn our language.

I don't know what I was thinking. I knew once he heard this, it would become a household saying whether I liked it or not. He had already picked up a lot of our cultural colloquialisms from other people who told him these phrases in secret as a prank on me, like someone who has taught a toddler to swear.

"Return with honor," he shouted one day as I left the house for work.

I stopped, dead in my tracks, and instantly felt a twitch run through my right eye. "What did you just say?"

The next Monday he texted me out of the blue: "Remember who you are and what you stand for."

Soon afterward, he asked me to help him dig out a rosebush in our backyard. After nearly an hour of hard labor, I collapsed into a chair on our patio, sweating and panting. He placed one sympathetic hand on my shoulder and whispered, "I never said it would be easy. I only said it would be worth it."

Since he apparently had been picking these up from somewhere to assault me on occasion, I figured he might as well learn my personal favorite, and that's when I told him about being thankful for the moisture.

"Why not just call it 'rain' or 'snow' or, I don't know, 'precipitation' if you're feeling fancy?" he asked. "Why 'moisture'?"

I told him I couldn't possibly give him an answer to this. No one could. It was one of those sayings that came from nowhere and became a part of our DNA. Utahns don't even hear themselves when they mutter it. It comes out as naturally as the breath that carries it. I was pretty sure the last time someone said it consciously, prophets were growing beards instead of condemning them.

"We're thankful for the moisture" is hardly the only of these prayer pleas that have turned into robotic mindless chants over time. It falls right up there with blessing the "refreshments and all the hands that prepared them" or bowing heads over the dinner table to ask that the food "will nourish and strengthen our bodies." These entreaties can be eliminated from one's vocabulary but only through hypnosis—and perhaps with the assistance of certain essential oils.

Once I told my husband about the "moisture," he became obsessed with this phrase, sometimes saying it in front of people who didn't know he was being facetious.

"We're sure thankful for the moisture!" he shouted to a neighbor one day. The neighbor politely nodded. I made a note to go over to that house later to explain.

"You need to stop worrying so much," he told me when I begged him to please not say this to people anymore for fear they might think he's making fun of them, or worse, that he's being earnest. "This kind of cultural stuff is fun and wholesome. I think it makes Mormons more endearing."

He's sincere when he says he finds this all delightful. Every time he learns a new harmless quirk about the culture around my childhood religion, he perks up.

He has shouted "we're thankful for the moisture" at me for

several years now whenever it rained or snowed. When I complain about him saying this, he shakes his head and whispers, "the Lord never gives you more than you can handle."

I don't know who taught him that one.

In March, we arose one morning to yet another massive snowstorm. *The Salt Lake Tribune* had already spent the winter reporting on our record-breaking season, and I was finding myself more and more often waking up in a bad mood.

With a groan, I pulled on my boots and trudged out to our wintry tundra to begin my painful descent down the driveway with a plastic snow shovel. An hour later, I retreated inside to warm up. My husband was sitting next to the fireplace, a steaming cup of tea in his hands, grinning ear to ear.

I glared at him. "What?"

"We're thankful for the moisture," he said.

"Are you?" I vented, shaking snow from my hair.

"Yes," he responded. "With every fiber of my being."

# That's How They Do Things at Their House

There's a common misconception outside of the Jell-O Belt that all Latter-day Saints are roughly the same. That, as a whole, the religion is packed with a mass of homogenous doe-eyed Osmonds who have never tasted anything spicier than a banana.

It may be true that if you put a thousand members of The Church of Jesus Christ of Latter-day Saints in a room together, you'd see some patterns (and a lot of filler and Botox), but the levels and ways in which one's devoutness manifests can vary drastically.

These variations in gospel commitment probably don't seem like much to those on the outside, but for anyone who has ever spent any significant amount of time as a citizen of Zion, the differences are stark.

As a child, if I ever found out a friend of mine was permitted to do something that was forbidden in my home, like play sports on Sundays or listen to explicit music, I would complain to my parents about this. They'd usually respond by saying something like, "Well, that's how they do things at their house, and this is how we do things at ours." There was no judgment in it. Just a simple acknowledgment that every family is different and sometimes ours was just more lame than someone else's.

I like to describe my own Latter-day Saint upbringing and family as the kind that almost never actually did Family Home Evening, but we also were the kind that felt supremely guilty about that. We were the type who drank caffeinated sodas but never turned down a church calling. We didn't go shopping on Sundays, but we also didn't attend church while on vacation. We weren't like the family down the street who got dressed up to watch General Conference in the living room and went to Nauvoo and Kirtland for every family trip. But we also weren't like that other (wicked) family who sometimes went boating on Sundays and let the kids watch *The Simpsons*.

Quick note: The inconsistency in my parents' rules around which television programs were prohibited during my childhood should honestly be studied. If a character of an animated TV show said "damn" one time, it was forever banned in our home. But we also regularly watched gritty prime-time procedurals as a family without batting an eye. When I was 7, my mother announced one day we were no longer allowed to watch *Care Bears*, an animated TV program for toddlers, citing some vague content-based reason. A few years ago, I asked her if she remembered what she found so morally objectionable about *Care Bears*, and she responded in a tone like she was finally ready to let me in on a family secret. "Oh, honey, I just couldn't handle one more second of that obnoxious theme song."

Mine is a full-tithe-paying sort of family. Well, excluding me. When *The Salt Lake Tribune* showers me with the outrageous sums of money I get for writing my columns, I immediately spend it all on babes and booze without even considering setting aside 10% for the Lord.

Mine is a family that goes to ward activities and stays after to help clean up, but not the type to volunteer for the choir or perform in the ward talent show. When I stopped going to church a decade ago, my membership records somehow got transferred to my childhood ward, so I started getting a lot of ward emails asking me to come in for tithing settlement or some other thing. I was finally dropped from the email distribution list when the ward activities committee sent around a Google document asking people to sign up for the talent show and I booked my 70-year-old parents to do comedy magic in drag. (My parents and I have never once discussed this incident, but these people raised me to be this way so I can only assume they thought it was funny.)

Even in my extended family, there were substantial variations in how we practiced the religion.

I experienced my own personal hell when I was 10 and was sent off to spend the weekend with my cousins who were the 6 a.m. daily-scripture-study type of family. After sitting through three hours of church that Sunday, I was informed that part of keeping the Sabbath holy in their house included wearing our ties for the rest of the day. We also weren't allowed to watch TV, besides *Saturday's Warrior* and old VHS tapes of past General Conferences. I hugged my parents extra hard when I next saw them. This was around the time someone at church told my dad if he didn't shave his beard, he would never be called as bishop. My dad responded, "Promise?" (He still has never been a bishop.)

Looking back, I'm not sure as a child I really knew what to make of the fact that a shared religion could produce such different rules for different people. Was my family made up of godless heathens or were we too buttoned-up or were we, perhaps, the perfect Goldilocks "just right" kind of Latter-day Saints? That's not a question anyone can really answer, even though there are certainly people reading this who already have.

For Easter 2024, my in-laws flew in from Portland, Oregon, for a weekend visit. My husband and I took them to my parents' house for a large family dinner with all my siblings and their children. After dinner, my dad read several New Testament passages and then led the group in a religious discussion about the meaning of the holiday.

When we returned to my house after the dinner, we opened a bottle of wine and sat in my living room, where my husband's non-religious parents commented that they had never really participated in a religious Easter celebration like that, asking me if that was a common occurrence with my family.

Warm memories from my childhood of singing carols at Christmas and attending ward activities flashed through my mind. Family prayers where my dad would take the opportunity to reference each of his children individually and tell God the specific reasons my parents were so proud of us. Quiet Sundays my family would spend together, playing card games after church and declining invitations from friends to go out and play. There was the boring stuff, too, and the aspects of the faith that are the reason it's no longer mine. But when it comes to my kind of Latter-day Saint family, it's the happy stuff I most remember.

I must acknowledge, even though I no longer practice the faith,

I have a lot of nostalgia for some of those times. Certainly not enough nostalgia to introduce these traditions in my home, but nostalgia even still.

I sipped my wine, thinking of my parents, and told my in-laws, "Well, that's how they do things at their house, and this is how we do things at ours."

# Pioneer Children Sang as They Walked

About every six months for the past 34 or so years, my mom has referenced an incident that happened in church when I was only 5.

Mom, a Brigham Young University music performance major, was never shy about belting the hymns during sacrament meeting, an affront to my tiny sensibilities in the late '80s, when one day I reportedly shouted to a quiet congregation at the conclusion of the opening number, "Mom, pipe down! You're embarrassing me!"

"This was during his 'phase,'" my mom will sometimes say, referring to a period from age 4 to 14 when embarrassing the family during religious gatherings was part of my routine.

Today I tell my parents these were character-building experiences for them, and I say it in a tone like I'm still waiting for a thank you I'm afraid will never come.

My most memorable outburst occurred when I was 6. My sisters and I had been assigned special speaking parts for the upcoming ward Primary program, aimed at celebrating the sacrifices of the Mormon pioneers as they traveled across the plains burying Cabbage Patch dolls that died during the journey (assuming our experiences later as teens attending stake trek activities were accurate).

The plan was that I would go to the microphone and say, "Pioneer children walked all day and never complained." This would then prompt the Primary to begin singing one of the classic bangers: "Pioneer Children Sang as They Walked (and walked and walked and walked)."

Even as a child, I recognized this as parental propaganda; this wasn't really about the pioneer children (who, no doubt, complained a lot). This was about us. The entire purpose of this portion of the program was to give our moms and dads fuel in a future fight about obedience and compliance. "Remember how you just

learned in church that pioneer children didn't complain? Now imagine what they would think of the way you're behaving over being told to clean up a messy bedroom."

The moment I heard about my assignment for the program, I told my parents I would, under no circumstances, be participating in this. They pleaded. Begged. Bartered. Did everything they could. But I was a stubborn child, and the more they pushed, the more I dug in my heels. Finally, my mother reasoned that maybe I was just scared to take the stage alone, and so she offered to walk up to the podium with me when it was my turn to calm my nerves.

This was offensive. I wasn't scared—just obstinate. But, at some point, I relented and agreed to my mother's proposal. And then my 6-year-old brain, which did not yet have the capacity to understand the concept of "consequences," came up with a quite terrible plan to teach my parents and all the adults of our congregation a lesson.

The day of the big program arrived. When it was my turn, I marched to the podium in my smartest black suspenders, my proud mother trailing me. I, freckle-faced and barely more than 3 feet tall, stepped onto a stool and pulled the mic closer to my mouth than necessary. I yelled my line, loud breaths between every second word: "Pioneer children walked all day and never complained!" The adults in the congregation were pleased with my conformity. I could see it in their eyes. I had pleased them with my chipmunk voice and blue clip-on bow tie.

My mother turned to walk away from the mic as the accompanist began the polite intro to the song. But I did not leave the mic. Instead, I pulled it even closer to my mouth like a drunken lounge singer and yelled, as loudly as my little voice would allow, "and THAT, ladies and gentlemen, is the stupidest thing I have ever done in my entire life." And with muffled snickers ringing through the chapel, my mother's back still turned to me, I jumped off the stool and slapped her behind.

There was an echo from the slap. It was louder than the congregants' gasps.

This story is still referred to, decades later, as "The Church Butt-Slapping Incident" in hushed voices among my family members.

I was thinking about this experience this past December, when my parents called to invite my husband and me to attend their sacrament meeting the upcoming Sunday, when my dad would be giving a talk about family. My husband and I aren't religious, and I hadn't attended a Latter-day Saint Sunday service in years.

"Absolutely no pressure," my mom told us. "We certainly understand if you don't want to come."

As I prepared to decline, my atheist husband, who had never before attended a Latter-day Saint sacrament meeting, whispered to me, "Obviously we're going," before saying the same out loud into the phone.

The day arrived and we donned our Sunday best and traveled to my childhood meetinghouse. We found my mother waving in our direction from a center pew, where she had saved a place for us. My husband sat up straight, singing, listening, participating, while I slumped next to him, scrolling through Twitter on my phone. He even took the sacrament (after asking me whether I thought the teenage boys breaking the bread at the front of the congregation had washed their hands). I tried to stop him, but he waved me away in a "when in Rome" sort of way.

When my dad took to the podium to speak, my husband

excitedly grabbed my mother's hand like they were proud parents who were about to see their toddler's dance recital. He even nailed the polite church laugh at each of my father's mild jokes.

As the closing hymn concluded, my mother singing at least as loudly as the rest of the congregation combined, he turned to her and said with the utmost admiration, "Cathie, you really carried this place on your back today."

I never was the son my parents deserved. Instead, I married him.

# Life's Guarantees

In fall 1991, I accidentally punched Simon Jones in the face during recess. Blood gushed from his nose like a faucet, prompting shouts from the other first grade eyewitnesses who then would go on to debate the level of intent behind the erratic swinging of my arms during whatever nonsensical game we happened to be playing at the time.

Noticing the commotion, the recess aide (a neighborhood mom tasked with ensuring we didn't kill ourselves or one another on the playground) rushed to Simon and guided him and his upturned face to the school nurse.

Seeing myself now as a fugitive who soon would be accused of scholastic crimes, I fled the scene, opting to hide in the boys' restroom, reasoning that since my teacher was a "girl," she wouldn't be able to find me there. Minutes later, as I stood on a toilet in the middle stall, I watched Ms. Beckstead's inch-long fingernail slide into the crack at the door and pry open the lock. I then was marched to the principal's office, Ms. Beckstead squeezing my wrist and practically dragging me (this was before children had any rights).

Over the next few days, I was summoned to the principal's office a couple of more times as a part of what turned out to be a relatively thorough investigation. Simon, of course, was willing to take the witness stand, but his story was not enough, alone, to convict me, since he couldn't speak to my intent.

Ultimately, my explanation that this had all been a misunderstanding apparently was accepted by the judge and victim, and the entire event was resolved with a lecture and a handshake. My parents were not called, which caused me temporary relief, soon replaced by an all-encompassing dread and guilt that I was supposed to fess up to them on my own. I was sure if they happened to find out I had been called to the principal's office through anyone else, they would escort me to prison for not telling them.

This is one of those predicaments that highlight how unequipped children are to properly diagnose the degree to which something actually matters. Looking back now with a moderate level of adult wisdom, I can see that it would have been perfectly fine for me to casually say to my parents, "I accidentally bumped a kid today and gave him a bloody nose, and I felt bad about it, but fortunately he's okay and the principal just told us to be more careful." Even if they were in bad moods at the time, this sort of disclosure wouldn't have raised an eyebrow for ol' mom and dad.

Although I already had been exonerated by the proper authorities, I was convinced I could be tried again, this time through my parents' criminal justice system, which I believed, based on personal experience, to be a much harsher jurisdiction than the one at Heartland Elementary School. This was mostly due to the number of times my mother had washed my mouth out with dish soap, which I'm positive didn't have FDA approval whenever my sisters told her I had said "damn" or "hell."

I decided to think about it for a day or two and come up with the best way to tell them. Maybe if I practiced it in the mirror a few times I could polish the speech enough to include all the correct adjectives to sell my parents on my innocence.

Days turned into weeks. Weeks turned into months. Before I knew it, a full calendar year had passed. I was now a second grader living on borrowed time. A second grader who regularly went to bed with my stomach tied in knots over the great and terrible secret of my depravity still locked away in the recesses of my likely irredeemable heart.

I'll take this brief moment to give a word of advice to any parents out there who are raising a highly anxious and guilt-ridden child: Most kids need to see a disappointed frown every now and then. Your kid is different. Start every morning by whispering to them in the gentlest voice you can conjure, "There is nothing wrong with you." Otherwise, they may turn into an insecure humor columnist who publishes embarrassing stories about your family without permission.

Consumed by fear, I finally reached a breaking point one autumn evening. I asked my surprised mother if we could go for a walk so I could talk to her about something. My heart raced as I opened my mouth to get out the words, resigning myself to whatever consequences awaited me.

Tears rolled down my red-freckled face as I explained I had been called to the principal's office for my role in the brief bloody brawl. The relief I felt to finally come clean caused me to abandon the more tempered version of the story I had practiced for more than a year. I even volunteered the part about hiding in the boys' restroom from my prowling teacher.

I have a lot of clear memories of interacting with my parents as a small child in the early '90s. Most are funny. Few are as tender as this one.

As I finished my story, I looked up at my beautiful young mother, who now had tears as well. My heart sank further as I realized I had done something worse than anger her—I had disappointed her and made her sad.

"Honey," she gently said, squeezing my arm, "we shouldn't hurt people. But you seem to know that, so I'm not worried about you." I fell into her arms and sobbed away my relief.

Perhaps defying a stereotype often assigned to overly sensitive gay men like me, I've never really considered myself to be a momma's boy. We love each other, no doubt, but this isn't one of those relationships that includes daily phone calls and matching outfits. And I'm sure I'm far from being my mother's favorite child, mostly because I can't compete with my three angelic sisters. Plus, I swear too much. And since we no longer live together, she has a much harder time washing my mouth out with bad soap.

But hot damn. Kind parents are not one of life's guarantees, and it's never been lost on me that I'm lucky.

# Jr. Jazz

In 1996, I was recruited for Junior Jazz basketball. That makes it sound like I had athletic talents and was discovered. In reality, an acquaintance of my parents told them they were looking for another boy to join his kid's team, named "Redwood."

At age 12, my sports history was already checkered. This included a couple of years of T-ball. The only photographic evidence my family has of my T-ball career is of me holding two doughnuts, my participation trophy tipped over and neglected at my feet.

Then there was my short stint in machine pitch—evidence of parental malpractice, considering they signed up their 8-year-old to swing at a flying ball after having never successfully hit an immobile one off a tee.

Eventually, I joined my neighborhood friends in a soccer league. We lost every game. My best friend, Sam, and I would sit in the middle of the field and make our team play around us while we gossiped about pop culture. We're both openly gay now.

So, no, it didn't make sense to sign up to play on the Redwood team. But sign up, I did.

I never became particularly popular among my teammates, and I'm certain none of them ever learned my name. I can't blame them. I wasn't exactly an asset. I spent every practice and game like I was in a dodgeball tournament, simply trying to stay out of the way.

As the season concluded, I felt relief—no longer would I have to dread Saturday games. But as our participation trophies were passed around, so too was a sign-up sheet for the next year. I must have misinterpreted my teammates' enthusiasm as peer pressure because I then registered to be on the Redwood team again, much to the surprise of my parents who, having attended every game, were also counting down the days until this nightmare was over.

The second year of Junior Jazz went like the first. And when

that season ended, I asked one of my teammates whether we were going to sign up for a third year. He told me no—the Redwood team was splitting up.

I was so elated that I skipped all the way home. Home was a mile away. That made this the most athletic thing I had done in two years.

But mere weeks later, a neighborhood child from our failed soccer team called me and said he wanted to pull the old crew together for Junior Jazz, and since I had already played for two years, he thought I should be team captain.

Flattered, and delusional, I accepted, and began my third year of Junior Jazz.

Unfortunately, on my new team, I was an average player. During games, my friends and I would fight over who had to sub in next, and we would regularly beg the coach to pull us out as we ran past him on the court.

The coach was Jake Anderson's father. He didn't know anything about basketball. He mostly just had us engage in team-building exercises, so our practices looked less like children in a basketball league and more like ropes courses for corporate employees.

We lost every game. In fact, the score would be so abysmal by halftime that the refs would simply announce we had forfeited.

When the season's final game arrived, we were thrilled we had only one more day of this embarrassment.

Inside the gym that morning, we looked across the court to the team that would be beating us. I noticed those players were shooting hoops. I noticed they were huddling around their coaches, receiving instruction. And then I looked more closely and realized these boys were familiar.

This team, the one we'd be playing that day, was my old team. The Redwood team.

Those players had told me they were splitting up. Evidently, they failed to explain they were only splitting up from me.

The lies. The betrayal.

As I looked at these, mine enemies, traitors, my dramatic gay little heart concluded I had no choice but to beat them. Yes—this was going to be the day I finally played basketball.

I called my friends into a huddle and explained the situation. They gasped. And we all decided we were going to destroy the Redwood team for what it did.

Four minutes later, we were losing 20-0. I realized I couldn't rely on my friends to help here, so I made a new plan: We wouldn't win, but I'd at least score one basket to show the Redwood players the talent they had shed.

For the next several minutes, I did something I had never done before. Instead of treating this like a game of dodgeball, I began running toward the ball to try to get my hands on it. It was very difficult. And before long, I was sweating. It made me wonder if this was why my old teammates were always so wet after every practice and game.

Finally, with the score now 40-0, the ball happened to fall into my hands. I was standing behind the 3-point line, a nearly impossible shooting position for me. But I knew I was not competent enough to dribble the ball into easier territory, so this was my only chance. And with my eyes shut, I launched the ball upward and forward.

The ball flew toward the hoop in slow motion. It seemed that every person in the gym fell silent. I felt the drama, the looks of shock from my former teammates, the surprise from my parents in the stands. The ball slowly descended and descended and descended toward my retribution and vindication until, finally, it fell straight through the hoop.

I began a victory lap around the gym before the ball hit the ground, screaming and reaching out for reluctant high-fives from the stands. When I finally returned to my teammates, still standing on the court and staring at me, one of them yelled, "Eli! You scored for the wrong team!"

Apparently, I did not realize when the ball fell into my hands, we were on the other team's side of the court.

The buzzer rang, announcing halftime. The refs declared we had forfeited. The score: 43-0.

After three long years, I finally scored a basket for the Redwood team. The only problem: I was no longer a member of that team when I did it.

We were sent through a long line to shake hands and congratulate the Redwood team on its victory.

When I approached the last child, the one who had told me the prior season the team was splitting up, he reached his hand out to mine. I prepared to confront him about his lie. But he spoke before I could.

"Do I know you? You look familiar."

# Singing Nuns

My childhood best friend was a boy named Sam. We met when we were 9 and discovered we had compatible imaginations that didn't seem to match those of our peers.

We'd make up games. The rules were not consistent, and the points didn't matter. Most of the games involved various reenactments of some prime-time television series geared toward adults, which we nonetheless watched.

We did pretend to be superheroes on the playground but not in the way of most of our contemporaries. This was the mid-1990s and the popular soap-adjacent series *Lois & Clark: The New Adventures of Superman* was airing on Sunday evenings. Instead of imagining we could fly, Sam and I would reenact dramatic dialogue-heavy scenes between Clark Kent and Lois Lane. (We always fought over whose turn it was to play Lois.)

By far our favorite role play involved *The Sound of Music*, wherein we, I'm sure to the silent objection of our family members, sang in hyperbolic operatic voices "How Do You Solve a Problem Like Maria" but altered the lyrics to include at least a touch of potty humor.

It was around this time that one or both of us had the idea that we should dress up as nuns for Halloween. We presented this plan to our fatigued mothers who didn't have internet access or any other reasonable way to procure a costume that no other 9-year-old in 1995 had even thought to request.

"Are you sure you don't want to be, oh, I don't know, a skeleton? Or a ghost?" they pleaded with us.

Nevertheless, we begged. Yes, we begged our Latter-day Saint mothers to turn us into nuns.

Sam's mom cornered my mom that Sunday in the church foyer. "Do you have any idea how to make a nun costume?" she whispered.

That's me on the right, mid-song. Sam on the left is about to call Maria a "flibbertigibbet."
Courtesy Eli McCann

"I've sketched out some models," my mom told her. "But I don't know. Maybe we can brainstorm and figure this out?"

Over the next few weeks, I'd peek my head into my mother's sewing room to find her hunched over her Singer machine, running a black piece of fabric under the pulsating needle. Piles of temporarily abandoned projects were scattered about this woman, who certainly never expected her decades of exceptional crafting experience to be channeled toward turning her 9-year-old son into a holy drag queen for all our South Jordan neighborhood to enjoy.

Finally, sometime around the end of October, Sam called. "Is your nun outfit ready?" He sounded giddy. "It's perfect," I told him, standing in my habit at the exact moment that my mother, on her knees and with a number of pins sticking out of her mouth, adjusted the hem in meticulous professionalism, taking this as seriously as if this gown would soon be on exhibit at the Met.

Our school invited us to wear our costumes to class on Halloween. Princesses, superheroes, ghosts and ninjas walked among us, as Sam and I tucked our hands into our tunics and marched in solemn character, elated to finally be living this dream.

We didn't view our evening of trick-or-treating as a quest to collect candy but rather a fulfillment of our civic duty to perform. To entertain. To dazzle.

With the recent popularity of Whoopi Goldberg's *Sister Act* to add to what Julie Andrews had already given us, we had enough music in our repertoire to fill out an entire album.

We marched from home to home, performing each tune, straight-faced and with excessive vibrato, before accepting any confectionary offering from the homeowner. Before long, neighbors began calling other neighbors to let them know Eli and Sam, the singing nuns, were on their way, and to be sure to make time for us. By evening's end, our reputations had so preceded us that entire families were answering their doors to give us a proper audience.

Our parents had received phone calls throughout the evening—neighbors giving their enthusiastic reviews and asking whether there was any way the show could get an extended run.

We couldn't have been prouder of ourselves.

The spectacle was such a hit, we reprised our roles the following Halloween for our last year of trick-or-treating, before puberty would begin to rob us of the innocence and self-confidence of childhood.

This next reveal may shock you, but Sam and I came out as gay in our 20s, long after the habits no longer fit, long after we retired our drag queen careers.

Shortly after we came out, I was talking to Sam's mom about our nunning days and I facetiously asked if she was surprised we both turned out to be raging homosexuals. She looked at me with such care, tilted her head slightly, and mumbled, "There were signs."

There were signs.

We couldn't disagree. And considering those signs, there's a piece of me that is baffled, and even a little proud, that in our conservative 1995 Utah town, our mothers' only hesitation in turning us into nuns was that they didn't know if they were up to the textile task. That our classmates didn't bully us but instead asked us where we got our cool hats. That neighborhood moms and dads didn't merely accept our flamboyance but shepherded us up and down our streets, with glee—never demanding we stop and instead requesting an encore.

In 2024, Sam and I both became dads within just a few weeks of each other. We now live in different states but have remained as close as brothers in the 30 years since we donned our gay apparel that 1995 Halloween.

Shortly after the birth of our sons, Sam and his husband, Travis, came to Salt Lake City to visit Sam's family and show off their infant. While they were in town, we took an evening to introduce our newborns to each other, even though at that point they were still essentially potatoes.

"Do you think they'll grow up to be best friends?" one of us asked.

"Do you think they'll have our odd imaginations?"

"Do you think they'll one day ask us to figure out how to turn them into nuns for Halloween?"

I don't know the answers to those questions, but sitting there, looking at our sons, I couldn't help but think the response to each might be yes.

If we're lucky.

# A Large Green Pillow

My great-grandmother's basement was filled with dusty Ball brand jars of liquids in muted colors with floating vegetables or fruits suspended inside.

The year "1991" was scribbled across the caps in black ink, signifying these delicacies from her backyard garden had been preserved several years ago, before being relegated to her musty storage room in the Salt Lake City home my great-grandfather built with his bare hands in the late 1950s.

"We have a lot to learn from grandma," my mother told me when I was a young boy as we stood in front of her jars.

"Self-sufficiency and frugality are very admirable attributes," mom said a week later as I helped her scrub two boxes of pickling cucumbers in our kitchen sink. I would spend the rest of that afternoon stuffing my face in a large green pillow in our basement in an attempt to escape what I thought at the time was a rancid smell coming from a boiling pot of vinegar, mustard seed, pickling spice, garlic and fresh dill.

The prior week my parents had devoted an entire Saturday to simmering sauces they had made from the hundreds of Roma tomatoes I helped pluck from our backyard just next to the chicken coop, which terrified me because it attracted rats and because the chickens were mean. Our steam canner was practically sacred, a symbol on our family crest, making its debut every June and sitting atop our stove until at least mid-October.

"Kids," my mom used to shout from the kitchen. "I need one of you to run to the storage room and bring me two quarts of crushed tomatoes and a bag of macaroni noodles."

We would venture into the basement, as requested, pulling a cord to turn on the light in our own personal Costco. We would pass by dozens of jars of apricot jam, applesauce, sliced peaches and salsas, all of which had been inventoried during a family night when my parents told us that a modest effort to follow our church leaders to maintain some food storage was a priority.

I balked when they explained we would be making a family trip next Saturday to an apple orchard to collect a few buckets of Gala apples for that weekend's project.

"I know you don't love this," my dad shouted over the sounds of our electric wheat grinder hard at work on the kitchen countertop. "But, in this family, we all pitch in."

"I hope you'll still do this when you're grown up and have a family of your own," my mom told me in 1999. I was a teenager by then and had just been tasked with chopping the ends off hundreds of strawberries.

"I really doubt this is ever going to be my thing," I told her. "I hate canning."

She sighed. "Well, that's okay. I know this isn't for everyone. I just hoped you would take to it eventually."

By the time I moved out, I was convinced my canning days were behind me. And I was right.

For a while.

Then, around age 30, a dormant strand of my DNA kicked in. I didn't even remember riding my bike to the farmers market, but suddenly there I was, lugging 50 pounds of produce through a crowd of people who looked just like my parents at 8 a.m. on a Saturday morning.

It seemed like Ball jars started spontaneously appearing at my home in the days to come. I swear I don't recall buying them. The canning life chose me like deity anointing a king.

Last fall, I walked into my house with a box of pickling cucumbers and a bag of fresh dill. My husband saw me and sighed. "Again?" It was more complaint than question.

"Self-sufficiency and frugality are very admirable attributes," I responded, interrupting his insistence that we had enough pickles to last several more years—given that we had barely made a dent in the 20 quarts I had canned the previous September, and given that neither he nor our dogs even like pickles (and I merely tolerate them).

When he first moved to Utah, I told him about the strong

cultural pressure to store food and the related pioneer impulse to preserve a lot of this food from scratch. He loved the concept when he heard it.

"But I really don't think we'll survive long on tomato sauce and apple pie filling if the apocalypse happens," he said as we stood in front of our packed basement shelves.

I shushed him.

He ultimately surrendered in his pickle protest as I started measuring white vinegar and dumping it into a large pot. Just when the concoction started to boil, I called my 69-year-old mother on speakerphone to ask her a question about how much dill she typically uses.

"I'm so glad you're canning again," she said. "We aren't doing much this year. It's hard to get through the supply without children at home." Her voice sounded a bit sad at the end.

"I should probably pull back myself or even take a break altogether," I explained. "We really have to force ourselves to eat everything I preserve each year. But it just wouldn't feel right not to see the steam canner on the stove every summer and fall."

I could almost hear her smiling through the phone. Just after we ended the call, my husband said, "I do love that you share this with your mom. It obviously makes her happy and proud, and she's more than earned that."

It probably was from the vinegar, but my eyes misted as I stirred the pot.

"I'm glad you're coming around," I told him.

Out of the corner of my eye I saw him cough and then stuff his face in a large green pillow.

# *Oh, South Jordan!*

In 1989, my mother was *voluntold* to make two dozen children's penguin costumes. She had a month to do this and no pattern, an obstacle she, master of the craft, likely considered trivial—this wasn't her first rodeo, so to speak. She had been commissioned countless times before to donate artistic labor through her sewing machine for her ward's upcoming theatrical pursuits.

Our stake had scheduled a roadshow, a staple of Latter-day Saint communal artistic expression in the 20th century, one which seems to have since fallen victim to cultural modernization and a concerted distancing from the "peculiar people" moniker of yesteryear.

Roadshows were as much a part of my childhood as anything else ever was. They were original stage productions, written, directed, and acted by Latter-day Saint congregations, by my memory lasting around 10 minutes each. Congregants were tasked with every aspect of the low-budget presentations, from costume design to staging to music to lyrics and even, yes, to dangerous acting stunts.

The most ambitious plays involved the largest casts, which often bravely featured young unpredictable children. Ideally these productions were supposed to incorporate some aspect of Mormonism and teach a religious message through a traditional three-act story arc.

No part was too small. At least, that's what they told us when I was cast as tumbleweed number four in our ward's 1995 loose parody of *Oklahoma!* (Our play was called *Oh, South Jordan!* and included such lyrics in the titular number as "Oh, South Jordan, where the wind goes sweeping 'cross my yard!") "You'll need to practice your cartwheels," Sister Jensen told us while measuring our limbs for the costumes on which she planned to sew a number of sticks. "I want the audience to almost feel the wind as they see the tumbleweeds rolling across the stage."

I'm not sure who came up with the penguin idea in 1989. My dad recorded the performance on our home video camera. I watched that recording dozens of times, and it was never really clear to me why our ward had made a play about penguins or what they had to do with, well, anything.

In the penultimate scene, the 24-penguin cast formed a semi-circle on the stage and performed a rap that was so offbeat and confusing that if I saw it now in any other context, I would assume it was brilliant ironic performance art. In the musical number, the penguins snapped in near unison as each took turns chanting, "I'm going on a mission and I'm gonna bring my [fill-in-the-blank]." The penguins shouted things like "scriptures" and "testimony" and "faith." The punchline of the scene: the smallest child, in what must have been something of a *Sound of Music* "So Long, Farewell" rip-off, saying, "I'm going on a mission and I'm gonna bring my . . . my . . . my teddy bear!"

This was a crowd-pleaser. Comedy gold.

But it wasn't enough to win the competition. Oh, I forgot to mention, the roadshow was a competition. After each ward in the stake performed its play or musical, a panel of judges would select a winner and runners-up. No tangible reward was given for the victory, but everyone wanted to be a part of the winning ward for complicated social reasons none of us could have explained.

"I don't understand how we lost to the Sixth Ward," my mother said on the drive home. She was referring to the winning one-act play involving a young woman on one side of the stage writing Dear John letters to all her missionary boyfriends who filtered in and out on the other side of the stage reacting in despair as she read them out loud.

"They didn't even have costumes," my mother muttered under her breath.

"The set design was sort of lacking. Furniture from the bishop's office?" Dad offered in support.

My sister said she heard two of the three judges belonged to the Sixth Ward, a scandal that was referenced with some regularity in my neighborhood for the better part of a decade thereafter.

We had a handful of chances, year after year, to best the Sixth

Ward after our failed penguin offering. We never quite got there. The *Oklahoma!* knockoff play was the last ward production in our South Jordan stake in 1995 and it, too, was a loser. By decade's end, no one really talked about roadshows anymore. I'm not sure if they just naturally waned in popularity or if there was a concerted corporate effort to end the practice, but as far as I'm aware, they are a thing of the past. An odd, cringey, bizarre cultural exercise that strikes fear in my heart when I occasionally worry there might be video evidence of my own embarrassing brushes with Deseret thespianism floating around in the world somewhere.

Having been out of the church now for more than a decade, I see these kinds of dead traditions through a much different, and often cynical, set of eyes than I did in the '80s and '90s. "Why were these ever popular?" I sometimes wonder, remembering these productions were typically hoisted upon the backs of what must have been exhausted neighborhood parents the same age I am now. I can't imagine why these volunteers would have been so willing to donate their limited time to something so cheap and cheesy.

Last summer, I ran into the mother of a neighborhood kid with whom I grew up. Now in her mid-70s, she stopped to chat, having not seen me in nearly 20 years.

"You know what I was thinking about the other day?" she interrupted me at one point. Her face lit up and she smiled. "Do you remember when you kids did that roadshow about South Jordan? Wasn't that a riot?"

I could almost see into the past through her damp eyes as she beamed at me—there, possibly amid her most precious memories, a community of neighbors rehearsing a bad play together, laughing, singing off-key, united in something harmless and wholesome. Something that would manage to become part of the fabric of us—the fabric that meant we were all from the same place, however peculiar and sometimes saccharine.

"Oh yes," I told her. Through my mind flashed a quick image of my friends and me getting jabbed by costume sticks as we rehearsed sloppy cartwheels behind the lead performers running through a chaotic square dance. On the other side of the church gym, the director was rocking her crying baby. A gaggle of neighborhood dads in jeans trying to start a game of basketball were intermittently interrupted by meandering children, too young for a roadshow role but dragged to the building by their parents who were involved with the production and couldn't find a babysitter since all the usual options were busy with cartwheels and square dances.

I smiled at my old neighbor over our shared memory.

"I'm so glad we did that."

# We All Have Jewel

Sometime around the mid-1990s, I began hearing regular speculation among my Latter-day Saint friends and neighbors that comedian Steve Martin was a member of the church.

I think it started right after his starring role in *Father of the Bride*, a 1991 film so white it wears neck pillows in the airport.

He wasn't the only clean-cut celebrity to be so labeled, albeit through unverifiable rumors spread by my Utah community. Tom Hanks. Angela Lansbury. Even Mandy Moore was baptized at 8, or so I was told by a friend who was moved by *A Walk to Remember*.

We didn't have the internet then. No quick Wikipedia search was available to undermine our confident whisperings. Not that Wikipedia would have deterred us anyway.

"It's not super well known, and he is really private about it," a boy in my Sunday school class told me in 1995. "But my cousin lives in Las Vegas and she said Gladys Knight invited Puff Daddy to church once and now he goes every week."

When I was 10, my friend Jackie's mom told my mom that someone in her sister's ward recently visited Graceland and had an amazing experience.

Apparently, just as the tour group was leaving Elvis' bedroom, the guide quietly pulled this woman aside and said, "I don't know why, but I just felt impressed to tell you that when Elvis died, they found a Book of Mormon on his nightstand with a bookmark at Page 422." We then looked in our own copies. HE WAS IN THE MIDDLE OF 3 NEPHI.

We rode that high for a year.

Conversations about which celebrities were rumored to be meeting with missionaries occupied much of my childhood. I rarely saw even the smallest inklings of dissent when someone made a claim.

Why would I or my friends protest any of this completely unverified information?

Maybe we couldn't say with certainty that Bob Saget was once a bishop. But we also couldn't say with certainty he wasn't once a bishop.

Eventually we grew up. The world changed. It seemed the most outrageous of the rumors—maybe due to the internet—became less common.

And then I sort of forgot about this part of my childhood.

*"I heard Mitt Romney hasn't gone to church since about 2005?"*

I was so informed 10 years ago at a dinner party. I had recently stepped away from my religion and my friends who had also left The Church of Jesus Christ of Latter-day Saints suddenly started saying stuff like that to me. They brought up well-known members and through attenuated citations insisted these people were living a different life privately than the one proud members knew publicly.

---

*Eli interrupting here: After the publication of this column, former Sen. Mitt Romney took to social media to post, "I am a true-blue member of the Church of Jesus Christ of Latter-day Saints. Ann and I attend sacrament meeting every Sunday and enjoy service in the temple. We love our church and the callings we have received in our home ward. A poorly sourced article in* [The Salt Lake Tribune] *that said otherwise is laughable. By the way, if you'd like to learn more about my religion, I'd be happy to help you meet with our missionaries—including some of my grandchildren!"*

*I woke up with messages from my family and friends (and many an angry stranger) who were intrigued that I had provoked Romney's ire.* Tribune *senior religion reporter Peggy Fletcher Stack reached out to Romney that day for comment, noting that based on his reaction it wasn't clear Romney had actually read the column that had annoyed him. After all, the article stated that this was "untrue gossip." To his credit, upon reflection and after being educated on the context of the reference to his name in this piece, he responded, "Ah, satire: 1. Me: 0."*

---

*"My classmate's cousin is a bartender and she has seen Donny Osmond at the Beerhive Pub."*

It was harmless, untrue gossip, probably not meant to be taken seriously, with the claims hardly interrogated and the names dropped casually.

It wasn't difficult to get used to this sort of thing. These conversations felt familiar. This was my childhood happening in reverse. This new group was undoing the stake-claiming I had participated in in the 1990s, using the exact same means and methods.

*"Marie Osmond left the church, like, 20 years ago but just hasn't publicly announced it because she doesn't want to lose her fan base."*

What I always assumed was totally one-sided gossip by eager Latter-day Saints was actually a quiet competition. Warriors were being claimed in this fantasy football-esque religious war. Celebrities young and old. Politicians. Philanthropists. No one was off-limits.

Tom Hanks called church members who supported California's Proposition 8 "un-American" in 2008. Many Latter-day Saints were horrified at the time. A notable victory for the disaffected.

But as the gentiles successfully identified their spokespersons in the early 2000s, the Saints became more deliberate, and factual, in their campaigning. "I'm a Mormon" ads popped up on my social media feeds, featuring D-list celebrities demonstrating it's possible to both do genealogy and be cool.

The war raged on. Our state's faithful continued to tag known celebrities, like Ken Jennings, while the others undermined the claims by pointing to Chelsea Handler (rumored to have Latter-day Saint roots). No one is officially keeping score, but the points feel about even.

It's easy to get caught up in it. But occasionally I take a step back and wonder why we do this.

As a kid, I guess there was something comforting about implausible stories of shared faith. It felt less lonely, if not validating. Why wouldn't those who left the faith feel the same way?

*"I'm not doing this by myself. The second set of footprints in the sand belong to Aaron Eckhart."*

That's just a theory. I guess I'm not really sure why, exactly, rumors about Sandra Bullock's faith made us feel more confident in our own upbringings in 1994. Why we implicitly valued her supposed judgment, sometimes more than our own. Why Ryan

Gosling not going to church anymore makes us feel more at peace about our similar decisions.

In his 2018 book *Calypso*, David Sedaris writes about waking up the day after the 2016 presidential election. He was deflated because of the results.

"Staring at the ceiling, wide awake," he writes, "I suddenly think of Cher and realize that what I'm feeling, she's feeling as well. . . . The next morning I wander the city in a daze, my eyes bloodshot from lack of sleep, thinking, I'm not alone. I've got Cher."

Maybe here, in Utah, we don't have the market cornered on the tendency to hope someone well known shares an opinion with us on something we care about. Maybe it's just human nature to claim warriors in our most treasured ideological battles.

David Sedaris has Cher.

In Utah, we have Steve Martin, maybe. We have Mitt Romney, possibly. We have Steve Young, depending on the topic. We're not alone. We all have someone.

In a perfect world, we all would have one another. Groups of people with different beliefs and experiences, supporting one another instead of relying on a stranger in Hollywood to do that for us—caring more about the people we actually know, different as we might be, and less about, say, whether a famous stranger was reading his scriptures when he died.

Getting there would take time, of course, and some humility.

Until then, we all have Jewel.

# Pissing Matches

It was sometime around 1995 when the dads in my South Jordan suburb got really into Magic Eye posters. You might remember the craze. Stores around the country began selling large prints of colorful patterns that, with some focus and patience, could reveal basic 3D images.

I don't know what exactly launched the interest. It seemed like overnight the mustached men of our neighborhood began plastering the walls of their homes with framed copies of the latest optical illusions. They would call one another whenever they acquired a new one and invite the other dads over to gawk and admire it, like they had secured an authentic Monet.

They all supported one another in word, but make no mistake, this was a pissing match. A confusing, guttural, almost subconscious quiet competition. A low-stakes battle to outdo one another.

"Did you hear Bob got his hands on a 12-by-8 print of the shipwreck?" we might have overheard someone say at church on Sunday.

"Oh?" another man would respond with a slight air of superiority that only the most seasoned in Mormon mannerisms could ever recognize. "He went with the small size, then?"

Eventually, Magic Eye posters were replaced by fish tanks. The fish tank craze was a decidedly more expensive and inconvenient hobby. But it did free up the wall space so the neighborhood moms could again display those Latter-day Saint temple photos and outdated family pictures with children in Easter dresses and mullets.

There were two ways to one-up a neighbor in the fish tank war. The first was to buy the largest fish tank available. The tanks were measured by gallon size, and this was the information the dads would lead with when announcing their latest acquisition. The second way was to purchase an unmanageable number of these receptacles in various sizes, placing one to three of them in each room of the house. Several of our neighbors' homes essentially became aquariums.

The fish tanks had to be cleaned once a month by hose to nearly empty them and refill with fresh water. My dad regretted getting sucked into the testosterone-fueled peer pressure the first time he had to do this with the 50-gallon tank that took up residence in our family room for the rest of the decade.

Tank size and quantity weren't the only status symbols worth bragging about. The tanks were filled with exotic fish—the rarer the better. Strewn about the base were artificial coral, half-buried miniature shipwrecks, and, for the tackiest dads, clamshell-brassiered mermaid figurines.

As a '90s tween, I joined the army of my contemporaries in feeding the neighborhood fish whenever a family went on vacation. That is, until one unfortunate episode in which I had forgotten about the new eighth tank in the Morleys' basement, and they returned from Disneyland to a rotting swamp of decaying rainbowfish. (I can't confirm whether this really was the reason my low-paying career in fish-feeding ended, but I've always assumed the reports of their death were greatly exaggerated, and it was for this reason I was never asked to be an aqua shepherd again.)

I assume the boomers of South Jordan moved on to a new collective hobby after the fish tanks, but I grew up and moved away before I could ever bear witness to it.

I've chuckled over the years thinking back to the Magic Eye posters and the pride they summoned from my dad's friends. What an odd thing in which to root one's self-esteem. And why would they feel superior to one another based on the size of their living room fish tank?

I suppose men have always been this way. When the first caveman met the second caveman, I'd bet my house the first thing they did was compare bone clubs and patronizingly compliment one another.

A few years ago, my husband and I got hooked on houseplants. We raided plant stores weekly, looking for anything colorful or distinctive. Before long, every surface in our house was covered with greenery, and I suddenly found myself tacked with a relentlessly time-consuming chore to keep them all on life support.

I realized what we were up against long before my husband did and began protesting new acquisitions, shouting "when will we have enough?" each time he brought home a new plant. He eventually had to start sneaking in plants and then gaslighting me when I noticed them, assuring me the new plant had always been there and expressing surprise that it took me this long to notice.

Some people have to find empty liquor bottles hidden throughout the house to discover their spouse has a problem. For me, it's receipts from Cactus & Tropicals.

I had to admit there was something thrilling about inviting friends over and giving them an unsolicited tour of our indoor forest.

"You're in luck," we found ourselves saying. "The Christmas cactus is in bloom. Two months early this year."

A few weeks ago my husband came home from a friend's house he had just visited.

"Brian has a lovely little olive tree planted in a pot on his kitchen table," he told me. "It's about a foot tall—makes a nice centerpiece."

"Oh?" I said, looking over at our own olive tree, which was about to outgrow our house, an involuntary smirk growing on my face. "He went with the small size, then?"

# White Shirt Army

A flustered man with a half-tucked-in, buttoned-up shirt, pit stains on both sides, paced past the church pulpit in the dark chapel, fiddling with equipment that seemed to be glitching. Flashes of livestreamed video were projected onto a large white screen behind him. At the bottom left corner of the screen, we could see a countdown timer announcing the conference session was set to begin in less than four minutes.

Cold metal chairs had been set up behind the 20 or so rows of padded benches in the main chapel area, extending all the way through the gym and underneath two basketball hoops. Someone had pulled apart the accordion doors that normally separated the chapel from this space. Another someone (with significant upper-body strength) would be assigned the impossible task of pulling them back and fastening them together once the chairs had been stowed away underneath a stage and the venue had been cleared.

My dad fished out a plastic container of Tic Tacs (the orange kind) and shook it in my direction. His wordless offer was accepted, and I held out my tiny palm to catch a few.

We were sitting somewhere toward the front of the metal chair section, our row full of my uncles and male cousins who had coordinated their joint attendance of this Saturday evening session of the 166th Semiannual General Conference. I watched my friends and their dads walk into the room to fill in the last of the chairs not already occupied by white-shirted Latter-day Saints who every six months would spend a Saturday night congregating in meetinghouses across the world to listen to sermons from Salt Lake City geriatrics, broadcast by satellite, and intended only for males ages 12 and up.

This October General Conference priesthood session of The Church of Jesus Christ of Latter-day Saints would be my first, having just turned 12 only five months before.

We watched the screen as prerecorded Tabernacle Choir music that had been playing in prelude was cut and cameras in the Salt Lake Tabernacle moved toward a pulpit decorated with every flower that could be plucked from the Wasatch Front. The background behind the pulpit fell dark and lights illuminated the evening's designated conductor, who then welcomed us by reading from a teleprompter that scrolled through some simple prepared remarks.

Two hours later, my yawning relatives and I shuffled into a couple of vans to try to beat the religious throngs to the nearest restaurant serving ice cream. It was already filled with white shirts when we arrived.

This would be our routine, every six months, for years to come. Coordinated attendance. A row stuffed with my extended family members. Ice cream down the street with the other male residents of South Jordan.

Our pack's numbers would ebb and flow as cousins left for two-year missions and then returned to rejoin our dutiful family quorum who tuned in to listen to church leaders who were periodically swapped out, thanks to mortality. The messages would remain largely the same. Missionary service. Education. Home teaching. The chastity lectures would prompt red-faced teens in the room to put their heads down.

Eventually, I left for my own mission, to Ukraine. I received a letter from my dad a week or two after my first General Conference abroad. "I attended priesthood session with my brothers and your cousins last Saturday," it said. "But it was lonely. I miss you."

I returned from my mission after two years and, like my cousins before me, I fell back into the fold. My dad paraded me around the congregation just before the priesthood session began like I was a soldier who had returned from war. He had called me earlier that week and left a message on my phone when I didn't answer because I was in class at Brigham Young University. "No pressure," his message had said, "but my brothers and your cousins will be going together this Saturday night, like we always do, and I would love to have you join us if you can."

Every six months for the next several years, I'd make the drive on a Saturday night from wherever I was living to join the crew in my parents' church meetinghouse, the same scene on display each time: a flustered man with pit stains fiddling with finicky audio systems. New generations of 12-year-olds watching their friends and dads enter and find their seats on the cold metal chairs. My own dad parading me around to his neighbors. My cousins, some now with their own 12-year-olds sitting by their sides, in white shirts, shaking plastic containers of Tic Tacs to drop a few into their children's hands.

Eventually, I broke away.

I went to the October session in 2013. Several weeks after that, I told my parents I was gay and that I finally decided it was time for me to step away from the religion of my youth. It was too painful to stay somewhere I really didn't belong.

A few months later, I got a call from my dad. "I totally understand if you don't want to come," he began. "But I just wanted to make sure you knew you were still welcome to go to the priesthood session with us. I don't want you to feel excluded."

His voice sounded casual, and I was sure that was a concerted effort.

"I'm not going to go anymore," I told him. "I appreciate you inviting me, but that's just not something I'm going to be attending from now on."

He was gracious, and we changed the subject. I hung up the phone with a pit in my stomach. Then I started a new biannual tradition: Every six months for the past 10 years, I've brushed off a tinge of sadness and angst at the vision of my father attending a meeting without a son to parade around to his friends.

A few years ago, on a Saturday night, my husband and I were driving to a gathering as we passed a Cold Stone Creamery, packed with at least two dozen boys and men in white shirts. My husband, a recent transplant to Salt Lake City, suddenly looked puzzled.

"Why," he said, "is everyone in that Cold Stone dressed like Mormon missionaries?"

I chuckled, and explained that these were fathers and sons who had just gone to a church meeting together—one that happens every six months—and that it's sort of a tradition to all go get ice cream together afterward.

"Did you used to do that with your dad?" he asked.

"Yes. And with my uncles and cousins. For years."

We were quiet for a moment as we drove on. Finally, he mumbled, "That sounds pretty nice, actually."

My voice cracked a little when I said it.

"Yeah, it sort of was."

# Please, Please Win

In 1992, MTV premiered a new television program called *The Real World*. In it, producers cast a handful of young adults who didn't know one another to live in an outrageous mansion together for a few months and drink themselves nearly to death.

For children of the 1990s, these hot young people—hardly older than us—were a televised testament that maybe we too could be trusted to navigate the complexities of adulthood.

The show's format and early seasons were particularly eye-opening for Utah Latter-day Saint teenagers, what with the partying and scandalous coed living. The unadulterated hedonism intrigued us while also allowing us to dip our toes into disrepute without ourselves becoming disreputable. *The Real World* was disconnected from our real world, filmed off in some distant land involving distant people with distant lives we could hardly understand. It was exciting in the way a lot of fiction is exciting. Aspirational, even if unrelatable.

Then Julie Stoffer showed up.

I was 15 when Julie, a member of The Church of Jesus Christ of Latter-day Saints and a Brigham Young University student, was cast for Season 9 of *The Real World*. There was a soft MTV ban in my home due to the network's proclivity, in my parents' view, to promote general hooliganism. But even they had to confess their own curiosity about a sister in Zion crossing the gritty airwaves of teen impropriety.

It's hard to explain how scintillating it was to discover a fellow Utah saint on MTV at that time. There had been a small slew of Beehive State celebrities through the years—usually of the Osmond variety—but we had rarely seen our faith and culture examined under such a worldly microscope.

And it wasn't like this Julie person was a former church member.

We'd seen those. We claimed them even while they disavowed us. But there was a limit to how connected we could actually feel to those who tried to hide the connection themselves.

Julie was an active Latter-day Saint, proudly claiming our lovely Deseret. She was a current student of the Lord's University. BYU wasn't her alma mater. It was her Alma. I don't know whether that joke makes sense. I haven't been to church since Mitt Romney was a presidential candidate.

The point is, my peers and I devoured Julie's season, salivating over every reference to our faith and state.

"Did you hear them talk about BYU in the last episode?" I remember my friend Tim asking. "They talked about her going to BYU."

We were embarrassed when Latter-day Saints on television were embarrassing. And we watched with a plea in our hearts that they represent us well. But even when they didn't, we couldn't look away.

Evidently deciding that "no press is bad press," the episode in which Julie's family visited and judged her fellow cast members over their partying habits and sexual orientation was like having fry sauce pumped into our veins. "Our parents would disown us," I remember one of Julie's brothers telling the gay roommate after wondering aloud what would happen if one of his siblings was gay.

One episode featured Julie talking with the BYU Honor Code Office about whether her broadcast turpitude merited expulsion. "She's just doing missionary work," my friend Nick argued. "Even Jesus hung out with the prostitutes and marijuana addicts."

The season ended, but the drama did not. Articles about Julie's ongoing consternations with BYU drummed up dialogue in our community. There were continued discussions about whether she did our faith a favor as she was suspended from school for living with men on television.

Julie's name had barely left our lips when suddenly, in 2002, Neleh Dennis was cast on *Survivor*. Premiering at the turn of the century, *Survivor* was structured around a social strategy game in which contestants were required to compete in challenges, forage for food, and "out-survive" other players.

Utah news outlets covered Neleh's assent in the contest like it was a presidential race. The coverage was exclusively positive. Neleh was cute. She was folksy. She was charming.

She was ours.

Every time Neleh uttered "oh my heck" it felt like our names were being individually read aloud on prime-time TV.

The neighborhood parents were less horrified by Neleh's coed living than they had been with Julie's. Maybe Julie had paved the way for Neleh, or maybe it's not really living in sin if there's no roof. Whatever the reason, Neleh was treated differently. She wasn't a controversy; she was a revered ambassador.

It was reported that Neleh had selected a copy of the Book of Mormon as a personal item to bring with her to the island. One of my Sunday school teachers cut out an article about this and read it to us, citing it as an example of missionary work coming in all shapes and sizes.

"Neleh could have brought *Teen Vogue*," Sister Swenson said. "But she didn't. She brought scriptures. Maybe that's why the Lord is helping her do so well on *Survivor*." We amen'ed that. We amen'ed the hell out of that.

Neleh truly was successful, outlasting nearly all the other contestants that season until she made it to the finals against another player named Vecepia. My entire extended family gathered at my Aunt Tami's house to watch Jeff Probst's live reading of the last votes. "Please win," I whispered to myself throughout the broadcast. "Please, please win."

We screamed in excitement whenever Jeff revealed a card with Neleh's name on it. We booed Vecepia. We didn't have any particular issue with the latter. But her success felt like a challenge to our way of life.

Neleh took second that season. She lost by a vote or two. I cried when it happened. I had recently come off two Utah Jazz finals losses to the Chicago Bulls. My heart could barely handle another Deseret defeat.

After Julie and Neleh, Utah's dabbling in reality television became more and more common, to the point that we eventually stopped noticing it so much. Producers pushed the this-might-be-a-sister-wife angle less in introducing characters, aware that the novelty had worn off enough that the general public wouldn't be intrigued to tune in just because a Utah Latter-day Saint was being paraded across the television like an exotic zoo animal.

It's funny to me now that we cared so much—as if my life or anyone's perception of Utah could ever change in any meaningful way just because David Archuleta nailed "Bridge Over Troubled Water" in the season finale of *American Idol* (another reality show runner-up from the Beehive State).

It doesn't really matter, of course. It didn't then, and it doesn't now. I know that. I probably kind of knew it then, too.

Still, even today, when a new set of characters is introduced in the first episode of my favorite reality programs and I find out one of them lives just a few miles from my house, I can't help but think from somewhere not very deep down, "Please don't be crazy. Please don't be racist. Please don't say 'oh my heck.'"

"Please, please win."

# Procrastinating Preppers

For as long as I remember, going back to the pioneer days of the late 1980s, my family had a semiannual tradition wherein we would perform a formal audit of our six backpacks with accompanying labels reading "72-hour kits." These were, of course, the front line of our emergency preparations, the product of some Sunday school lesson or televised prime-time public service announcement, or perhaps both.

Dad, as patriarch, usually would lead the session, passing out the bags to us four small children and my mother, who sat like the rest of us, cross-legged in a sacred family circle. Mom had a clipboard to keep notes—the taking of minutes was a volunteer activity, and the minutes were never again reviewed or approved, but they did lend a level of authenticity and gravitas to what might otherwise look like an inconsequential gathering of pajamaed Latter-day Saints on a Sunday evening.

We would begin combing through the kits' supplies, Dad retrieving item after item out of his own and asking us in order whether we could identify the same items in ours.

Matches. Flashlights. A confusing amount of hard candy, which mom explained was for "sustenance," chosen over healthier options because it could last forever without turning bad.

We would find and unfold ponchos, investigating them for rips. Dried-out tubes of lip balm would be opened and rubbed. There was always at least one item no one could identify. We would never throw it out because what if it was important?

Eventually, Dad would announce we were woefully unprepared for the looming natural disaster the token semiannual General Conference talk had warned us was nigh (without ever getting into specifics). Then we would repack the same stale supplies we had just audited and store the backpacks away near the 50 jars of applesauce that had been optimistically canned over the prior four apple-picking seasons. The 72-hour kits would be forgotten for the next six months.

"We'll get those updated," mom would periodically say. Then she would sigh, let out a yawn, and mumble, "Someday."

I don't know if we used this name for it back then, but gradations of the "prepper" lifestyle seemed to permeate my Utah community in the 1980s and '90s. For example, neighbors took the charge from Latter-day Saint leaders to maintain a two-year supply of food in their basements to varying degrees of compliance.

While some homes' basements were converted to bunkerlike environments, stashed with MREs (meals ready to eat), rifles and Bibles, our own was often the musty venue for dehydrated fruit and sleeping bags we never used. Ours was a family who only pretended to go camping.

The schools conducted fire and earthquake drills. The latter were more fun because they were typically infused with theater, our thespian vice principal using her voice and nearby office supplies to perform 60 seconds of chaotic sounds over the intercom while we covered our eyes and hid under our tiny plywood desks that were meant to protect us from a collapsing building and electrocution.

The combination of doomsday warnings received from church and state, both apparently unified on this topic, caused my best friend, Mandy Williams, and me to begin hoarding candy under her bed in preparation for an impending famine that never materialized. Our responsible attempts to prevent the mass extinction of the human race were thwarted when Mandy's older sister and her friends, fifth graders, discovered our supply and took care of it for us during a tween slumber party.

My propensity for emergency preparation carried into adulthood when I began canning my own applesauce that would never get eaten. So did the fire and earthquake drills, this time organized by my employer, during which an alarm would sound, prompting my begrudged co-workers to descend the stairs in our downtown high-rise to walk across the street and be head-counted by stone-faced Janet from human resources, holding a flag and clipboard and looking like she had waited her entire life for this moment.

By the time I entered my 30s, I began to feel all this preparation was for naught. Decades of emergency kit audits, food preservation efforts and drills had filled my brain and time with seemingly useless fearmongering propaganda and information, never to be deployed onto some disaster.

Then, suddenly, it was 2020, and a worldwide pandemic shut us in our houses and threatened to upset supply lines. Grocery stores were raided for toilet paper, pasta and yeast. It was like we were living in 1992 Russia.

We couldn't find bread.

"It's okay," I told my husband, Skylar, on day three of this. "That's why we have our emergency food supply."

I handed him a can of something I had preserved sometime within the past decade (my Sharpie-scribbled year on the cap was illegible).

"What . . . is it?" he asked.

"It should be food," I explained, to the very best of my ability. "And maybe some botulism."

Three days later we awoke to an earthquake.

Our century-old house swayed from side to side. As we started to comprehend what was happening, Skylar flew out of bed and began sprinting around the house screaming words our mothers don't think we know. I followed him, both of my arms flailing in the air, shouting all the obscenities he hadn't already claimed. Our dog ran circles around us, barking.

We didn't cover our eyes. We didn't climb under any plywood desks. We didn't go outside to look for Janet from HR and apologize for not taking her more seriously in the past.

Instead, we darted to the exact center of our home, stood under a heavy chandelier, and cried.

When the ground stopped moving and the rumbling dissolved into silence, Skylar looked at me and said, "What happened to all my training? I've participated in earthquake drills since I was 7 and all I did just now was run around screaming."

I thought of my family's 72-hour kits full of dead batteries and stale candy.

"We really should do an audit of our emergency preparedness supplies," I suggested.

“When?” Skylar asked.

I channeled my exhausted working mother, circa 1989, and mumbled an answer in a tone I immediately recognized as defeated.

“Someday.”

# Open-Mic Sunday

A number of years ago, my husband and I were having dinner with a friend when she started telling us about some drama that had unfolded during a sacrament meeting.

"A woman in my ward in the 1980s confessed to having an affair with a man sitting in the second row during a fast and testimony meeting to the surprise of everyone and people ended up screaming at each other in the pews. I don't know if this makes me a bad person," she said, "but that might have been the most entertaining day of church from my entire life."

My husband, unfamiliar with many Latter-day Saint terms, cocked his head and asked, "What's . . . fast meeting?"

"You ever been to open-mic night at a coffee shop?" I responded. "It's like that, except a good portion of the participants are children whose parents are whispering what to say into their ears and you frequently hear a full recounting of your neighbors' recent vacations to Disneyland or Nauvoo, Illinois."

"That sounds lovely," my husband said in sincerity. "Such an efficient way to catch up with everyone on the block."

I shook my head at him and explained further.

Mostly these meetings in The Church of Jesus Christ of Latter-day Saints include quiet personal sermons, certainly meaningful and perhaps even therapeutic to those participating, but nothing he'd find particularly interesting unless he was prepared to engage in a substantial number of sincere life and philosophical changes.

Even the most devout Latter-day Saint would concede, if they were being honest, that these meetings rarely feel like a party. The excitement—certainly to the extent of that shared by our friend over dinner—was the exception, not the norm. But anyone who has attended a good number of these has definitely seen some things.

There was a time while I was serving a mission in Ukraine

where we had to pause church services when a man attempted an object lesson from the pulpit that went awry, set off smoke alarms and caused at least one asthmatic attack. I don't remember the point he was trying to make, but he had brought with him a large box of matches to demonstrate what happens when you light all the matches at once. Other congregants who had been victims of his past presentations yelled at him, in vain, to stop as he pulled out the first match. The following Sunday, branch leadership reread a prior statement, printed on a tattered piece of paper, prohibiting the use of fire in the building. I made a mental note to seek out a local to find out more of the history on this. I don't remember whether I ever got any answers.

An uncle of mine called once, in amazement, to tell me about an elderly woman in his Salt Lake City ward who had "borrowed" a number of the orange flags placed at crosswalks for pedestrians to use to make themselves more obvious and visible to traffic. "These flags saved me, just like Jesus," she said, waving two of them high in the air and managing to preach a religious sermon and provide a public service announcement simultaneously.

"I can honestly say I'm more likely to use the flags now, thanks to her endorsement," my uncle added.

"But church leadership really does try to discourage this sort of excitement," I told my husband after recounting a number of these stories, explaining that I regularly heard reminders from headquarters about appropriate content for these meetings back when I was still a member.

He shook his head in polite disagreement. "That's the wrong move. If I was in charge, I'd tell people to get as creative as they want for these meetings."

This is typical for him—to suggest some constructive criticism about ways to liven up the religion a bit when he learns some new fact about it. He came up with a plan once that he swears he'll execute one day: He wants to put down a red carpet in front of a Latter-day Saint meetinghouse on a Sunday morning, dress in drag, and stand near the door with a fake microphone so he can ask people as they enter the building, doing his best impression of Joan Rivers, "Who are you wearing this morning?"

"Don't you think people would love that?" he asked. "It would be so funny."

I didn't know how to answer his question, and I'm still not sure whether to discourage him or to encourage him to have someone film it if he ever gets up the nerve. I tried to explain that I didn't think churchgoers would have nearly the sense of humor he was expecting if he ever did get around to doing this. But what do I know?

A few years ago, a friend invited us to attend her daughter's baptism. When we arrived, my husband greeted the family and asked how baptisms work. After someone explained the basic mechanics, he shouted, "How fun! I love swimming!" prompting laughter from those within earshot.

He brought a card and a small gift for the child, and as we sat with the other attendees waiting for the program to begin, he started jotting down on the card: "You were having an AMAZING hair day. Such a shame you had to get it wet."

"You can't write that," I whispered. "People take these things seriously—you might offend them!"

He waved me away with his hand and added both of our names to the card before sealing it in an envelope.

Later that afternoon, at an open house, the parents of the child read the card out loud, prompting sustained laughter from the rest of the crowd.

The child's grandmother clasped one of my husband's hands with both of hers, wheezing, and telling him, "You are just a riot!"

He beamed—a smart aleck who had found his audience.

Maybe they should put him in charge.

# A Jesus-Filled Christmas

It never occurred to me how religious my family members were until I saw my husband experience a Christmas with them.

Suddenly, I saw cultural traditions through his eyes, and they turned into foreign rituals to me, like the reading of Luke 2 and a screening of a film produced by The Church of Jesus Christ of Latter-day Saints with hot white people portraying the story of Jesus' birth.

"That was a lot of Jesus," he said to me on the drive home after one Christmas Eve dinner at my parents' house.

"Oh?" I asked him. "More Jesus than at Christmas with your family?"

He told me there was no Jesus at his family's Christmas. "Just wine and a lot of fighting, and usually in that order." Then we debated the correct amount of Jesus that should be a part of the holiday festivities, like we were discussing appropriate salsa spice levels.

"Well, it is a religious holiday," I reminded him.

We godless heathens are but visitors to their celebrations, cosplaying as believers on an annual basis to get presents. Certainly we can't expect them to accommodate us, here.

When I put it in those terms, he seemed to agree.

"I wasn't trying to be critical," he assured me. "I've just never really experienced anything like that before."

From time to time, I'll joke about his lack of familiarity with religion, since he was raised without any. His mother will protest if she's ever within earshot.

"My children weren't completely devoid of exposure to religion," she once told me. "I'm pretty sure we had a Bible somewhere in the house—or at least a copy of *The Secret*."

My husband once objected when he heard me assert that he never went to church growing up. "That's not true," he said. "I went to church one time as a kid, and I loved it. They had live music and mini-muffins and coffee." Then he paused, looked up as if hit with an epiphany, and muttered to himself, "Actually, that might have been a bakery."

By the time our second Christmas together rolled around, he seemed much more prepared for the religious celebrations. That is, until my family attended a live performance of Michael McLean's *The Forgotten Carols* on a Thursday night in mid-December.

"Here's what you need to know," I started downloading onto him on the drive to the concert venue. "A man wrote a musical in the '80s about various people from the New Testament whose stories never get told singing about the birth of Jesus. Like the innkeeper who has allegedly regretted his decision to reject Mary and Joseph and so now he takes the stage every year to remind audiences to 'Let Him In.'"

"And," my husband started to ask with caution, "this is, like, important to your family?"

"I don't know," I confessed. "Somehow we end up with tickets to this nearly every year. The tickets are like candy canes; no one is sure where they come from, but it would feel wrong if we didn't see them every December."

It was inconsiderate of me not to warn him about how the show ends, but I simply had to omit this part out of an interest in self-preservation. For the uninitiated: McLean concludes each of these shows by instructing audience members to hold hands with the people on either side of them, rock back and forth, and sing an eternal round of "we can be together forever someday." The most hurtful things I've ever heard my siblings say to one another have happened at these concerts when we all fight over whose turn it is to sit on the end of our set of seats and next to a stranger. Keeping my husband in the dark on this would ensure he didn't question the seating arrangement when we invited him to enter the row first and sit down next to the bearded man wearing an American flag T-shirt and cowboy hat.

After the two of them swayed together singing their eternal commitment for 10 or so minutes, my now-enlightened husband leaned over to me and whispered, "I was owed this information before we got married."

In the years since, he has adjusted more fully to these religious traditions, helping me arrange the Nativity sets my mother has given us, humming Michael McLean tunes while we decorate our tree, and singing at 70% accuracy the words to "Silent Night" with my parents on Christmas Eve.

He even persuaded my family to get tickets to *The Forgotten Carols* again this year. (Although he acknowledged he saw this mostly as a hazing opportunity for our new brother-in-law who has married into the family.)

His cultural ignorance still pops up here and there. He recently met Kurt Bestor at a fundraiser and hit it off with him in the corner of the room. He called me over after chatting with Bestor for a half-hour or so and said, "Eli, I want you to meet Kurt. He says he's a musician, and I think we should support him."

His education is ongoing.

Even still, this Christmas, we'll hang our secular ornaments like we always do. We'll video chat with his family in Portland, Oregon, over glasses of wine and get caught up on family gossip. And then, on Christmas Eve, we'll drive to my parents' house for dinner and a full biblical recounting of the holiday's significance, including immaculate birth reenactments by my most willing nieces and nephews in period costumes made out of old bathrobes.

As we leave to drive back home, my mother will hug us and whisper a half-facetious apology to my husband. "Sorry," she'll say. "I know you didn't grow up religious and would probably prefer to celebrate this differently, but we can't help ourselves."

"Please don't apologize," he'll respond, in absolute sincerity. "This was perfect."

# A Christmas Box Full of Garbage

Since I was a young child, my mom has recounted a Christmas story to us on an annual basis—her most memorable holiday.

This must have been around 1969. Mom grew up as the oldest of 10 children, raised by a terrific single mother, exceptionally poor. Christmas in her family was simple, and it rarely included any gifts to write home about.

When she was in high school, her younger siblings excitedly woke her up on Christmas morning, telling her there was a large, wrapped present in the living room with her name on it. Mom found the box a minute later. It was tall, up to her waist. She opened it and discovered the box was filled with trash. Mom figured her younger brothers were playing a mean prank on her, and she started to scold them for it, but they encouraged her to dig through the garbage to see if there was anything else in there.

Under the crumpled newspaper and discarded packaging, she finally found it—a brand-new sewing machine, something she had wanted for a while but could never possibly afford. She soon discovered her younger sister, Diana, had taken odd jobs around town and saved money for an entire year to buy it for her.

"I loved the gift," Mom has said to us through tears over the years. "But the sacrifice meant so much more than the sewing machine."

Mom learned to use that sewing machine and has since made enough clothes to outfit a midsize country. She became so good at sewing that she now belongs to a highly competitive quilting group that's harder to get admitted into than the Illuminati. One of my friends once asked my mom if she could possibly attend quilt night with this group sometime, and my mom laughed like the friend had requested casual access to Soviet state secrets.

Growing up in a family that had a certain "it's the thought that counts" philosophy when it came to Christmas gifts has left an impact on me. "Just be thoughtful" has been my motto. No need to go over the top.

Then I met someone who changed everything.

In 2015, I had just begun dating my now husband, Skylar. He was living in Wisconsin at the time, and so he would fly to Salt Lake City for periodic visits. One such visit occurred in early December of that year. I'm a lawyer by day and was in court when his flight arrived, so I told him he'd need to keep himself entertained for a few hours until I was done with work.

I didn't find out how he had occupied himself during that time until a few days later when I returned from the airport after dropping him off and I found, in my kitchen, a small envelope with my name on it. I opened the envelope and retrieved a card that had a riddle on it directing me to a nearby coffee shop, where I was supposed to ask for a woman named Sarah.

The next day, as instructed, I asked the neighborhood barista whether there was a Sarah who worked there. This barista's face lit up when she saw me holding the card. She ran to her purse and pulled out another envelope with my name on it. This new envelope had another card with another riddle, this time directing me to a nearby hardware store, where I was supposed to ask for Michael. Michael's card sent me to a grocery store to locate a Derrick.

The card-gathering scavenger hunt took me all over the city until, finally, the last card directed me to the location of my Christmas present, which, frustratingly, was hidden in my own house, mere feet from the location of the inaugural card.

I've told a lot of people this story and the typical reaction includes swooning gasps and an admiring "awe." Then I'll remind them this whole ordeal took me weeks to sort out and was, in fact, quite inconvenient.

But something happened as I went about my hometown gathering clues from strangers who recently had an interaction with Skylar: Each place I went, the summoned employee would hand over the card and then gush about how much they enjoyed talking with him. Several of them said some variation of "you are so lucky" to me. I realized he had gone about town charming everyone in his wake, to the point that they had become some of his most loyal personal evangelists.

The final present in my home was underwhelming, if I'm being honest. But the sacrifice and the bonus of hearing so much adoration of this man I had just begun dating were the real gifts—among my favorite gifts I've ever received.

He couldn't have intended it, but the effect of this experience was such that by the end of it, thanks in no small part to positive references from service providers across Salt Lake City, I was convinced that I wanted to marry him one day.

The tradition of clever and committed gift-giving has continued. It has made holidays in our home more fun, even if chaotic and disruptive. Remind me to tell you the story sometime about the year I, with a 102-degree COVID fever, deliriously adopted a puppy over the internet to surprise Skylar for Christmas. Word of advice: Do not surprise your spouse with Christmas pets.

But I digress.

Whether it be a garbage-buried sewing machine or an animal that will most certainly urinate all over your house and eat your new couch and not improve even after expensive intensive training, may the sacrifices embedded in your own expressions of love mean more than the stuff this holiday season.

And if nothing else, may your favorite gifts come with at least a small amount of torture.

# A Handful of Nuts

My great-grandpa Hinkle was born in 1906. By the time I came along, he was in his 80s and had begun a slow descent into Alzheimer's, which meant he would often greet us with a curt "who the hell are you" whenever we went for a visit.

On one occasion we were at his home for a Christmas party, where he suddenly shouted, "What's it going to take to get you people to leave?" His outbursts didn't often make sense, but looking back I can see sometimes he just said things the rest of us are too polite to utter.

My grandma (his daughter) once told me he was always such an odd guy that it wasn't often clear where his personality ended and the dementia began. Was his habit of passing his dentures around the room for his great-grandchildren to hold before popping them back into his mouth more illness or quirk? We never could say.

Because of Alzheimer's, Great-Grandpa would often repeat stories from his life, usually beginning again the moment the story ended. As a result, many of his anecdotes are so ingrained in my mind that they sometimes feel like they happened to me instead.

He would tell one story every Christmas when we went to his house for a visit. He never seemed to like the holiday. It triggered something in him, and I don't know that any of us ever got a full answer on what that something was. He would sit in the corner of the room, while the family visited and exchanged gifts, and just sort of cry. But at some point, he'd start talking, and tell us the story of his most memorable Christmas.

Great-Grandpa Hinkle grew up exceptionally poor in Council Bluffs, Iowa. He came from a wildly abusive home. On one occasion, one of the revolving doors of stepfather figures pulled a gun on him. That's the sort of environment that was the backdrop of this particular story.

He was around 13 years old, meaning this happened, I guess, right after World War I. Constantly on the verge of homelessness, he was living with his mother and siblings in a run-down hotel room, helping to scrape together enough pennies each week to keep the family somewhat fed and warm. This was a particularly frigid winter in Iowa, per his telling.

Members of his family didn't really celebrate Christmas because they didn't have money for gifts. It was easier to try to ignore the day and its annual reminders of their poverty.

That Christmas morning, his mother gave him whatever change she had and asked him to go down to the corner market to buy an item—in repeating the story, he never could remember what the item was. He set off to the store, passing the homes of families keeping warm and exchanging presents.

He arrived at the corner shop, bought the item he was sent to retrieve, and then stepped back onto the icy street wearing whatever rags for clothes he had used to bundle up. As he began to walk away, the store owner came outside and called for him. "He knew our situation," Great-Grandpa used to say as tears filled his eyes. "He knew what it was like at home."

Great-Grandpa turned around and paced back to the shopkeeper, who reached out and dropped a handful of nuts into his little palms. "Merry Christmas," the man said, before turning around and retreating into his store.

Great-Grandpa would sometimes say the handful of nuts was the only Christmas gift he ever remembered receiving, and the kindness from the shopkeeper, who apparently had little to spare himself, always stuck with him.

We tend to think about poverty, about homelessness, around this time of year more often than any other time. People struggle outside of the holiday season, of course, but, for some reason, that struggle is more on our collective minds as the snow falls and the wreaths appear on front doors.

Maybe the changing season and the dropping temperatures make it harder to not imagine what it might be like to have nowhere warm to go. Maybe the opulence of the commercial aspects of the holiday celebrations shine a subconscious light on the unfairness of relative privilege and the cruelty in the way it tends to skip a lot of people. Or perhaps the general spirit of giving that permeates December naturally causes us to think about who most needs to receive. I don't know.

Many years ago, a cousin of mine was hurting financially. She was a young single mom and as the holidays approached, my large extended family decided to throw a small party to collect funds to do a surprise Sub for Santa for her. She was invited to this party but was not told she was going to be the intended recipient of the charity. As the event wrapped up, my cousin handed the party organizer two dollars from her purse and said, "I hope this helps whoever this is all going to. I sure know what it's like to struggle."

I think about that every Christmas. About her impulse to help and how so often the most generous among us have the least to give. About how baffling it is that in our communities that are filled with people who have far more than two dollars to shed, there are perhaps just as many who could desperately use them.

No, I'm uncertain why we tend to think about these issues more around this time of year, but I do think the annual gut check has some value, even if it would be great if it happened far more often.

May it serve as a reason for reflection for all of us—a prompt that will get us to ask what we can give, collectively and individually, to those looking for a warm place to sit, and some humanity to go along with it.

Even if all we can spare is two dollars and a handful of nuts.

# Pioneer Day

In July 2014, I was living in an apartment on South Temple in downtown Salt Lake City when I started seeing families pull their minivans over to the side of the road and erect folding chairs on the shaded parts of the street's park strip.

"They're claiming their places for the parade," a neighbor told me. "This starts happening around this time every year."

"For Pioneer Day?" I asked, puzzled. "That's not for another five days."

The neighbor shrugged.

Having grown up in the Salt Lake Valley, I was, of course, familiar with Pioneer Day and was aware the downtown festivities included a large parade every July 24 (unless it fell on a Sunday). Although we never attended the parade, my family participated in the holiday each summer while I was growing up. Our celebrations mimicked the Fourth of July so a lot of my memories of this particular tradition are a bit blurry and hard to parse now. In fact, I don't think I knew these were two wholly separate and distinct holidays until I was at least 14. I just thought our neighborhood was so patriotic we celebrated Independence Day twice.

Five days after people started setting up their chairs in 2014, I walked out to my apartment balcony to watch the parade crawl its way down the packed street. I don't know what I expected to see. Cosplaying pioneers. Covered wagons. Brass bands belting out old-time Western folk classics. Any of that would have made sense, given that this holiday and the parade that kicks it off are meant to honor our exhausted, bloody-footed, migrant religious ancestors who trekked through the unforgiving desert plains and mountains to seek refuge in our sparse, salt-aired valley.

When I saw Santa go by in a motorized recliner, however, I realized we had really lost the plot on this whole thing. Or maybe it was the space alien-inspired float. Or the mermaid wearing a black skirt to cover her legs in an apparent attempt to make the fishtail coming off her heinie give the illusion that she was swimming down the street instead of walking (it did not successfully give this illusion). Or it might have even been the off-off-off-off-off-brand Winnie the Pooh throwing hard candy to tiny, crying spectators.

True, there were pioneer cosplayers. But they marched, in character, carrying a confusing and aggressive number of apparently prophetic 50-star U.S. flags, seemingly unaware the whole point of this holiday is to honor our frantic fugitive forebears who fled the United States to start over in this, our lovely Deseret.

Just as a covered wagon with the words "Salt Lake Granite Stake" plastered along the side made its way down the street, a loud cheer caught my attention, and that's when I noticed some raucous parade watchers a few balconies away. A sign from their railing read "Happy Pie & Beer Day." After a quick observation, it became clear they were taking that second part of that message very seriously.

"We love the pioneers," one man screamed, holding up a beer can as if to toast the paradegoers. A woman in a bonnet riding on the front of the wagon blew a kiss up to the tipsy spectators in response, prompting enthusiastic cheers from the drunken crowd.

Behind the wagon, a giraffe-themed float blasted "Wipe Out" by the Surfaris. To the side, sweaty marathon runners who had been funneled down the parade route to make their way to the Liberty Park finish line jumped over and dodged armies of obstacles, thanks to the many wandering toddlers whose parents had gotten distracted.

A float mounted with a large papier-mâché spider—and no other context—then came into view.

I stood there in awe, taking it all in on my balcony—the chaos, the festivities, the enthusiasm from beer-guzzlers and churchgoers alike, all of this in the quirky town I love to its core.

It then occurred to me it was a Thursday morning. The rest of the country was going about its business on this typical workday, oblivious that Salt Lake City essentially had shut down so thousands of residents could party with St. Nick, bonnets, beer and pizza. Later, fireworks would light the night sky as a broadcast down the street of muumuu-clad Tabernacle Choir singers belted out jubilant frontier anthems behind overeager cymbal bangers and trumpeters.

Soaking all this in, I chuckled and whispered to myself, "This holiday is a hot mess."

The images from that 2014 parade are seared into my memory. Every time I recall them, I smile.

My assessment of Pioneer Day hasn't changed in the past nine years. It is an absolute mess. A baffling, contradictory, somehow over- and underinclusive, and sometimes misguided curiosity. A Frankenstein's monster of a holiday, slapped together with unbridled and illogical traditions, symbols and activities, celebrated sincerely or sarcastically, and, for many of us, a little of both at the same time.

Yes, Pioneer Day is our state's most wonderful, if not embarrassing, punchline.

And I love the hell out of it.

# The Lone Cedar Tree

The year is 1847. Mormon pioneers are trekking toward the deserts of the Mountain West. Their new leader, Brigham Young, is on a quest to find a new plot of Earth, far away from an unfriendly government. He's modern-day Moses-ing hundreds of Latter-day Saints under the harsh summer sun.

On July 24, they emerge from a deep canyon, since named "Emigration" because of this event. Brigham looks at the bowl-shaped Salt Lake Valley in front of him, surrounded on nearly all sides by dramatic mountains. It is there he reportedly says to those close enough to hear him, "It is enough. This is the right place. Drive on."

The mountain desert landscape varies from the green and humid climate the pioneers had abandoned. Here they find finite snow runoff water and sagebrush.

One supposed standout: a large tree located not far from what would become the city's center point. Legend states this was the only tree growing in the valley, and it quickly became known as the "Lone Cedar Tree." A story would pass down that the pioneers wandered to that tree, stopped below its branches, prayed and sang hymns.

Historical accounts called into question the tree's "lone" moniker. One 1847 pioneer, John Young, wrote that when he entered the valley, he spotted "seven, wind-swept, scraggy cottonwood trees and one oak tree" not far from Lone Cedar.

Another account from September 1847 records Brigham Young cautioning settlers from cutting down trees along the creeks. In "selecting your firewood," he said, "it will be wisdom to choose that which is dry and not suitable for timber of any kind, and we wish all the green timber and shrubbery in the city to remain as it is."

Legend states, nonetheless, that the Lone Cedar Tree became

a gathering place for the new settlers. Couples got frisky in the shade. Secret meetings by political and church leaders (the Venn diagram was a circle) happened at the tree's base.

The tree eventually died, although no one seems to know when, including perhaps the tree's most loyal friend, the Daughters of Utah Pioneers (DUP), which was organized in 1901 with a mission of preserving history.

A 1924 headline in the *Salt Lake Telegram* read: "Old Cedar Post Object of Reverence; Daughters of Pioneers Take Interest; Fence to Protect It from Vandals."

"Seclusion and protection from an annoying world are rewards merited by old age," the article began. "Even a tree, in its declining years, would register objection to slaps and pats or the curious and vigorous jabs from sturdy but well-meant boots could it only talk."

The article explained that "some of the gravest secrets connected with the building of the great empire of Zion are locked up somewhere in its heart." (The writer seemingly had a word count target he desperately needed to meet.)

The dead tree was fenced and protected. In 1934, it was moved a short distance, into a center pavilion at present day 600 East and between 300 South and 400 South in Salt Lake City.

The shriveled stump sat under a cupola. A plaque placed at the base of the tree by the DUP stated, "Over this road the pioneers of 1847 . . . found growing near this site a lone cedar and paused beneath its shade. Songs were sung and prayers of gratitude were offered by those early pilgrims. Later, the cedar tree became a meeting place for the loggers going to the canyons. Children played beneath its branches. Lovers made it a trysting place. Because of its friendly influence on the lives of these early men and women, we dedicate this site to their memory."

The monument sat largely ignored until late at night on September 21, 1958, when vandals cut down most of the remainder of the tree and took it away, leaving a 20-inch stump. An outraged DUP President Kate Carter lamented how discouraging it is when "vandals come along and tear down our good work."

Soon after the disappearance, *Salt Lake Tribune* Editor Art Deck received an anonymous phone call, telling him to check a

Greyhound bus depot locker for the remnants of the tree. There he found a sack full of ashes—a mere ghost of the cedar.

No culprit was ever found.

Around this time, Russ Mortensen, director of the Utah Historical Society, privately mocked the attempts to preserve what he called a "historical fraud" and "a dead stump with little historical value."

When the *Deseret News* published his statements on what must have been a slow news day, it set off a contentious debate among historians about the truth claims surrounding the tree.

In 1960, the remaining portion of the stump was encased in a new monument, stuck on top of a concrete pedestal and placed under the cupola. Years later, the stump disappeared, having been sawed off the monument.

The remnants of a monument once cared for still sit in the 600 East pavilion. Weeds have sprouted through bare places. Old pioneer homes that face the decaying monument are continually being crowded out by rising apartment complexes.

In 2014, while house hunting, I visited one of these homes, discovering in it an old trunk, filled with century-old newspapers. From a small window, I could gaze down the street and see the top of the structure of the Lone Cedar Tree monument.

This house, and those surrounding it, would have seen the site of the crime. They would have seen DUP members gather there, perhaps in tears, nearly 70 years ago to mourn the loss of what to them mattered.

Today, the structure is rusted, picked apart and ignored by passing vehicles. The 1934 plaque is missing, having been pried from the pedestal that once supported the rotting wood of a tree that held pioneer secrets in its heart.

Near the pedestal is another plaque, dated 1960. It explains the other plaque in a way. A monument honoring the monument. Its language comes from a place of hurt and maybe even defensiveness. It's written by the Daughters of Utah Pioneers.

"LONE CEDAR TREE," it states in all caps. "Although willows grew along the banks of the streams, a Lone Cedar Tree near this spot became Utah's first famous landmark. Someone in a moment of thoughtlessness cut it down, leaving only the stump which is a part of this monument. 'In the glory of my prime, I was the pioneer's friend.'"

The old monument exists now perhaps less as an honor to a tree with a disputed history and more as a preservation of a 20th-century battle between historians. The tree, and then the monument to the tree, and then the monument to the monument, are like us: generation replacing generation, trying to preserve the story of its forebear, however imperfectly or inaccurately.

Each new event—and subsequent updated iteration of the storytelling—seems to accept the dwindling consensus that the origin story is significant or even true, but surely that doesn't mean we should stop trying to tell it.

# Thirty Recipes in Thirty Days

One of my most important pieces of dating advice for those interested in one day marrying is to find someone who enjoys doing the chores you hate. I'm convinced the surest recipe to a happy marriage is staggering the tasks you each despise.

When I found out my now husband enjoyed washing dishes and folding laundry, I put a ring on his finger so fast I injured him. On the other hand, it's been six years since our wedding, and I don't think he has ever learned how to start the lawn mower. Not long ago, he walked into the house in a panic and said, "Have we ever changed the furnace filter?" I told him, "Yes, every month for the past decade." I'm going to need someone to check in on him when I die. And please come help me set up our smart devices if he goes first.

I'm the resident cook in our home. My husband has no interest in helping. I'm truly fine with this because I enjoy the task. Unfortunately, for both of us, I'm not particularly good at it. But I make dinner for us every night.

My husband is polite so his review of the meal, when I ask for it, is typically something like "I'm just really grateful you made it." He sounds so sincere that I forget to notice he has refused to answer the question.

He once told me he was going to have "I didn't really follow a recipe" etched onto my tombstone, referring to my common refrain just before we partake of my vibes-only style of cooking.

I didn't grow up learning much about culinary arts. This is entirely my fault. My parents are both fabulous cooks. If we ever ate out, I don't really remember it. We were a household with a wheat grinder in active use. We had chickens and an embattled steam canner. Mom and Dad probably tried to teach me some of this self-sufficiency, but I was an unwilling student.

Mere days into my 2003 Latter-day Saint mission to western Ukraine, where I discovered neither I nor my first companion knew how to turn on a stove, I regretted having never learned to cook. We had a rule in our mission that we weren't allowed to eat meals with any church members so whatever food we consumed had to be gathered and prepared ourselves.

Every day my companion and I would buy a loaf of white bread and a small jar of raspberry jam and rip and dip with our bare hands, sitting across from each other in our Soviet-era apartment while rabid street dogs fought over a chicken leg outside the window. The only difference between us and them: We had to participate in companionship inventory every Wednesday.

After six weeks, I was transferred to another city with a new companion, who I learned also did not know how to cook and lived off oatmeal and chamomile tea. By this point, we both essentially had scurvy and an eye patch.

There was no way I could possibly live with straight dudes (who had the hygiene to prove it) for the next two years and also have to starve in the process, so I quickly decided I was, without internet or tutors, going to teach myself to cook something, anything.

I'll note here, quickly, that from time to time someone will ask me if it was difficult for me, a raging closeted homosexual, to live with straight men on my mission. I usually explain that the fact that I cohabitated with heterosexual teenagers for 24 months and still somehow came out of that wanting to date men is definitive proof that conversion therapy could never work.

But I digress.

I raided our apartment, hoping to find a cookbook. In a kitchen cabinet, I unearthed one—a dusty, laminated step-by-step guide to beginners cooking, prepared years ago by a former mission president's wife for someone in my exact predicament.

The cookbook contained 30 recipes. The instructions were so dumbed down I felt offended just reading them, even though they were exactly what I needed. There was an entire page dedicated to explaining how to turn on an oven. "Before you chop up the onion," a recipe warned, "you need to take off the skin. You don't want to cook or eat that part. You need to just throw that away."

I decided to cook my way through this cookbook, like Julie Powell did with Julia Child's *Mastering the Art of French Cooking*. Thirty recipes in 30 days. I'm still waiting for someone to option my story for a film. (I would like to be played by Meryl Streep because, well, she can do anything.)

It started with a simple spaghetti. The next day I made "pizza" by cutting a loaf of bread in half, spreading tomato sauce from a jar over the two sides, and sprinkling it with cheese before popping it in the oven for a quick broil (there was a long warning about how fast the broil function can turn into a disaster).

The recipes became slightly more complicated as I worked my way through the cookbook. I made a shepherd's pie. Tacos. Chicken soup. The 30th recipe was a large pot of nine-ingredient Ukrainian borscht. I was so proud of how that turned out I genuinely felt confident I was ready to star in a hit TV cooking show.

By the time I got through the book, I had learned the basics of cooking and was able to start branching out and even modifying or making up new recipes. And then something amazing happened: I started to find this new hobby, once intimidating and insurmountable, to be therapeutic and calming. It quickly became my favorite part of the day. Which, yes. The bar was low, considering that the rest of my day consisted of falling on ice and getting yelled at for pounding on someone's door to tell them the Lord can see them drinking their nasty green tea and to knock it off.

Cooking through the years since has become a big part of who I am, which is remarkable, considering that I've never really gotten much better at it. I do it because it calms me when I'm stressed, so I have no desire to push myself to improve because it seems like that sort of strain would defeat the purpose.

But no one is knocking down my door for a seat at my dining table.

Still, last week my husband was cleaning out a baking cabinet in our kitchen, where I store all the duplicative supplies I have inadvertently purchased.

"How attached are you to these nine bags of hardened brown sugar?" he yelled at one point. "Are any of them a family heirloom I should know about?"

I rolled my eyes.

"Seriously, Eli," he shouted, "why are there a dozen half-used identical cans of cooking spray in here?"

"You should be grateful," I yelled back, feeling a phantom imprint of a missionary nametag over my left breast and almost hearing the sounds of street dogs mid-fight. "You could be eating a loaf of bread dipped in jam for dinner tonight."

# The Gift of Tongues

Mere weeks after I returned to Salt Lake City from my mission to western Ukraine in 2005, I was recruited to volunteer to provide interpretation services for General Conference sessions of The Church of Jesus Christ of Latter-day Saints.

I learned that while there was a deep bench of professional native-speaking interpreters for such languages as Spanish and French, the church was desperate at that time for anyone in Utah with basic proficiency in Ukrainian.

That's how I, a supremely unqualified 21-year-old, who 24 months earlier couldn't have even pointed out Ukraine on a map, ended up sitting in a fancy booth at the faith's Conference Center in downtown Salt Lake City trying desperately to keep up with the translation of hours' worth of sermons.

I was hardly the first missionary to be dropped into the deep end on interpretation services. My sister likes to tell the story of a time she visited a Latter-day Saint sacrament meeting in Italy, where she was handed headphones to listen to the interpretation being offered by an American missionary who sat in the next room speaking into a microphone. During the meeting, the missionary went dark for several minutes while an Italian speaker at the pulpit rapidly mumbled through what my sister guessed was a long and convoluted story before finally pausing to look down at his notes. During the brief break, the missionary's defeated voice came through my sister's headphones, "Uh . . . I think he said something about a boat."

Growing up in Latter-day Saint congregations, I had regularly heard about the miraculous gift of tongues bestowed upon missionaries, a gift that supposedly enabled them to master a new language in a matter of weeks of fervent study at Provo's Missionary Training Center. Imagine my surprise several years later when I

"I THINK HE'S... INVITING EVERYONE... TO AN AFTER-PARTY..."

sat, wide-eyed and barely competent enough to breathe on my own, in a Soviet-era Kyiv apartment wondering why I didn't understand a single word of a conversation happening in front of me between a toddler and her mother.

The next Sunday I was invited to stand at the pulpit in sacrament meeting to introduce myself to the congregation, having just arrived in Ukraine that week. After the meeting, I asked my mission companion why I had been laughed off the stage after muttering the two or three phrases I had repeatedly practiced that morning. He looked at me with such pity, contemplating whether to let me know I had misremembered the word for "new." "Well," he said, "I think you really lost them when you announced, 'My name is Elder McCann and I'm horny. Fortunately, I've already met some of you, so I don't feel too horny. I'm grateful that you have all helped me not feel so horny.'"

"Don't feel too bad," a friend who had arrived in Ukraine the same time as me told me a week later, when I ran into him and shared my embarrassing story. "A few days ago I announced to an entire Sunday school class that I believe God murdered Joseph Smith."

A few weeks after that I was assigned to be the choir director for our small branch in Lviv. After our second or third practice, I dismissed the group by tearfully informing them, "I really enjoy sleeping with each of you every week. You are all so talented, and it makes me happy that we all get to sleep together after church." The choir was reduced to tears of laughter, and it took a minute or two for anyone to gain enough composure to explain to me what had happened. As we left the building to go home that night, a choir member put his arm around my shoulders and mumbled in broken English, "I think it will better if you more studying to speak."

"I think it will be better if I more studying to speak," I thought to myself in 2005 as I sat, white-faced and shaking, in the Conference Center's Ukrainian interpretation booth. Copies of the many talks had been emailed to us days in advance so we could practice, but the email came with a warning that it wasn't uncommon for certain elderly speakers to go off book.

It turned out I was right to be worried, or so I found out mere minutes into the conference session in which I frantically tried to keep up, frequently losing my place. A friend sat in the booth next to me, switching off with every other talk, performing about as well as I was.

The fatigue grew over the two hours of that morning conference session. I couldn't help but picture my Ukrainian friends on the other side of the world, listening to me massacre their beautiful language, no doubt remembering times I inadvertently propositioned them for sexual favors while adorned in a black nametag and a cheap, oversized, boxy suit.

I was fired from my interpretation job not long after this experience—I was told the powers that be had located enough native Ukrainian speakers to handle the work going forward, but I've always wondered if that was just a polite lie.

I stepped away from the church many years ago. Fuzzy memories of my short stint as a General Conference interpreter feel almost like an odd fever dream to me now—as foreign as they are funny.

Even still, I'm grateful I had that experience. It was humbling, and I probably needed to be humbled. It was fun and exciting, although intimidating and exhausting.

More than anything, it makes me smile to know that somewhere, out in the world, there's a video of an old man standing behind a pulpit speaking for a moment or two before my young, flustered dubbed voice interrupts and says in sloppy Ukrainian, "I'm so sorry everyone. I've lost my place. By the way, I miss you terribly."

# Mary Matt Drinks Coffee

I recently began my second decade as a coffee drinker, and yet I still can't walk down the coffee aisle at the grocery store without feeling like I'm in an airport.

The smell of a coffee bean transports me to some very particular place—an office building, a café, the home of that one non-Latter-day-Saint family on my South Jordan block in 1995.

This is because no coffee in any form ever passed through my childhood Latter-day Saint home in the 1990s, so I learned to associate the smell with certain places where I occasionally would encounter it.

Mom and Dad were strict observers of The Church of Jesus Christ of Latter-day Saints' Word of Wisdom—well, besides Diet Coke and Dr Pepper and Pepsi (which are not actually against the health code) and meat in moderation and other hot drinks that are not coffee or tea, unless we're talking herbal tea, which can be hot or cold, but green or black tea may not be either; also Red Bull is fine, of course, obviously.

Around 2001, we had a student from South Africa stay with us for a few days as a part of some kind of exchange program. When this young woman requested a cup of coffee, my mother frantically called Mary Matt, her Catholic friend, and whispered into the phone, "Can you please help me? I have no idea how to make coffee."

Fifteen minutes later, a groggy-eyed, frizzy-haired Mary Matt marched over to our house in her bathrobe with a steaming pot and poured a full cup for the student, like she was on a humanitarian aid mission.

Throughout my childhood, I heard Latter-day Saint friends say they wished they could try coffee because they liked the smell. This never really resonated with me—coffee always smelled to me like something was burning on a stove. This remained true for me through my 20s. I was never tempted to drink the stuff.

Then, in May 2014, I set off on a trip to Ukraine and Poland with my friend Brandt. We had both recently begun our exodus out of the church, and I guess that's why we were prepared to experiment with hard drugs, like a 12-ounce mocha or an iced organic jasmine green tea.

It was the day before my 30th birthday, and we stumbled into a hip underground coffee shop built into a cave, accessible only through a tunnel. Inspired by the atmosphere, I announced to Brandt that I was prepared to try coffee and, channeling my best Brigham, I spread my arms outward and shouted, "This is the right place."

Brandt agreed to join out of support, whispering to me, "But, like, what are we supposed to order? Can you just order 'a coffee' or is that like going to a restaurant and ordering 'the food?'"

I didn't know the answer to that question, and so, like my mother calling Mary Matt for emergency support, we rushed back outside and Googled, "How do you order a coffee drink?" A website gave us basic descriptions of popular beverages, and a minute later we walked back in and asked for two lattes and lots of sugar, please.

We sat, sipping, and asking each other, "Do you feel anything yet?" as though we had just snorted cocaine. And, honestly, coffee and cocaine basically seemed like the same thing to me at that time.

For the rest of the afternoon, we power-walked the streets of Lviv, Ukraine, like a gaggle of Draper, Utah, moms who just made a joint New Year's resolution.

Looking back, the boost in energy probably had less to do with the small amount of caffeine we had ingested and more to do with the incredible volume of sugar we had dumped into our drinks, making this less of a latte and more of a melted cup of coffee-flavored ice cream.

That trip began my long, ravenous relationship with hot caffeinated beverages.

I don't quite know how to explain this, but I was more nervous for my parents to find out I started drinking coffee than I was to tell them I was gay and no longer going to church. I had come out to them months before my trip to Ukraine. They were supportive—model parents, in that regard. I guess ceasing church attendance seemed justified, so that was easier to explain; I was gay and staying in the church was agonizing and unhealthy for me. My parents seemed to follow that logic just fine. But drinking coffee? Well, now I was just being disagreeable.

I finally ripped off the Band-Aid by asking for a latte at a coffee stand during a family trip to Disneyland as my parents stood on either side of me. It might be the only time in history a grown man has ever felt brave for ordering a drink from a teenager dressed like Dick Van Dyke riding a carousel in *Mary Poppins*.

I was prepared for a conversation—at least a few polite questions about my latest destructive lifestyle choice. But no conversation came. It turned out my parents are normal, well-adjusted people who don't spend energy thinking about how others choose to ingest their caffeine.

As we walked away from the coffee stand, I sipped my latte and suddenly remembered watching *60 Minutes* with my family in 1996. Mike Wallace had just asked then-church president Gordon Hinckley if it was true that the Word of Wisdom meant church members don't consume caffeinated soft drinks and Hinckley confirmed this. (The faith's official policy does not actually bar drinking caffeinated pop, though such thinking can still be found in church culture.) Hinckley's answer must have come as a shock to my devoted parents, who, at that exact moment, had Diet Coke pumping into their veins through an IV.

They didn't stop drinking their favorite beverage, and I don't remember them spending any time grappling with the topic after the interview, even as many of my neighbors hotly debated the issue for the next decade.

I guess my parents had already learned what it took me until my 30s to learn: Sometimes you just have to figure out what works for you and not stress about what everyone else thinks. People's consumption of the devil's bean really has nothing to do with the content of their character. After all, Mary Matt drinks coffee, and she's one of the best people we know.

# The Courage to Dream Big

I started coming out of the closet in 2014 at age 29. This was something I never thought I'd do, and I surprised myself when I finally built up the courage to tell my family.

Shortly after I began this process, I found myself in Bosnia, traveling with some friends who had two small children. They would go back to our accommodations each evening around 7 so they could put the kids in bed at a decent hour, leaving me to wander town alone.

Our first night in Sarajevo, I found out there was one gay club in the city, and I was curious to see it. When I arrived, I discovered the club was nothing more than a tiny basement room with a radio in one corner and a small refrigerator with a basket filled with cash on top serving as the bartender. A man acting as security guard at the door talked to me for a minute or two before he let me enter.

I grabbed a drink, dropped some cash in the basket, and parked myself on a stool in the corner of the room to watch the 20 or so people all mingling and listening to music. After a while, a young woman approached me and told me she wanted to introduce me to her shy friend, Anel. She waved him over, and he and I chatted for a couple of hours before heading out to walk around town so he could show me his favorite sites.

I learned that night that Anel had also recently started coming out to his family. He was soft-spoken and kind. He seemed almost traumatized, like he was carrying a massive weight on his shoulders. He told me being openly gay in Bosnia wasn't very safe at that time and that police or other locals regularly raided the club where we met. We ended up wandering the city until 2 or 3 in the morning, sharing our hopes and dreams and what it was like to live in places where a good portion of the community and lawmakers didn't think much of gay people.

For the next few days, I met with Anel around 7 each evening. We strolled the city, talking until early in the morning.

On my last night in Sarajevo, Anel asked me what I hoped my future would look like in a perfect world. I thought for a minute or two and told him I wanted to marry and have a family—that's what I had always wanted—but that I had never really felt like that was realistic. Anel's eyes filled with tears as he told me that's what he wanted as well. He then said something I've thought about for years: "It's hard to have the courage to dream big but the wisdom to dream well."

I understood him at that moment—he was engaged in a battle with which I was familiar. He was tempering his expectations, trying to have the wisdom not to expect that he could have an uncomplicated life with someone he loved.

Just then Anel realized how late it was and told me the last train back to his neighborhood was about to depart. He needed to go, but he wanted to show me something first. We took off in a sprint through the dark and empty Sarajevo streets, me following him, until we arrived at an old fountain. He asked me to take a drink. I did so. Then he interpreted the sign just to the side of us: "He who drinks from this fountain shall one day return to it."

"Now you're destined to come back," he said. "So this isn't really goodbye."

We both had tears in our eyes. He kissed me and darted off to hop on the train just as it was pulling away. I watched until the train was out of view and made my long lonely trek back to the apartment where I was staying.

I met my husband two months later.

I've shared this story with people through the years, and the most common response is that it sounds "so romantic." But that experience has never seemed romantic to me. It was cathartic. It was beautiful. It helped me to process three decades of constant onslaughts of homophobia that had nearly convinced me I was irredeemably broken and undeserving of happiness.

I returned to Salt Lake City from Bosnia, and our Pride festival happened a week or two later. I attended and saw a joyful community expressing love and support for one another, and I couldn't help but compare this with that dingy Bosnian basement club.

While my own community still had (and has) a long way to go in gaining adequate empathy and understanding for LGBTQ people, I did feel grateful for the progress that had been made up to that point—progress that allowed me a privilege not yet afforded to Anel: the knowledge that dreaming big and dreaming well sometimes can be the same thing.

# Bagpipes and Free Hugs

In the late 1990s and early 2000s, controversy swept Salt Lake City and The Church of Jesus Christ of Latter-day Saints when locals complained about a deal between the two entities to sell a portion of Main Street. The idea was to allow the church to develop it into a small plaza connecting two of its large downtown properties. There were various iterations of the arrangement through the years, carved up and amended due to threatened and filed litigation.

Ultimately, a federal appeals court heard complaints that converting the formerly public space into a private religious site with all the supervising and content restrictions that entails might violate the First Amendment. The court ruled the sale of the property to the church was constitutional and the matter ultimately faded from the public conversation. Most of this story is a distant memory now for those of us who were around to witness the fight. Everyone else likely assumes Main Street heading northbound always ended at South Temple.

I was a teenager when the city held one of its televised City Council meetings in which it had invited the public to attend and voice their concern or support for the proposed sale.

Latter-day Saints lined up to express their appreciation that this small section of Main Street was going to be put to better use, in their view. Another crowd—of what I'm sure I thought of as "antagonists" at the time—gave speeches about the right to free assembly and their discomfort with the idea that a government can sell important public property to the area's predominant religion.

Several critics who showed up to speak were familiar to me—loud, boisterous, bearded protesters I had spotted surrounding Temple Square before and after General Conference sessions. They usually hoisted large signs insisting conference attendees repent and start listening to Jesus, something the attendees no doubt believed they were already doing by going to conference. Some of these signs contained vulgar claims about church founders and current leaders. The most clever of them included large colorful drawings of the devil burning the wicked. (I always liked those ones.)

I don't know how long this has been a practice, but at least at that time, alongside the protesters, you could always find Latter-day Saint counter protesters, adorned in JODI dresses and Mr. Mac suits, singing hymns. Or holding up "free hug" signs. Or yelling back at the beards. Or (seemingly out to hurt everyone all at once regardless of creed or conviction) playing bagpipes.

The circus scene appeared to grow with each passing year. The battle to out-noise one another, probably counterproductive to the broadcast's administrative efforts inside the conference venues, didn't die down when sessions began. The sidewalks' various stakeholders stayed firm at their posts, continuing to shout down and drown out one another's attempts at screamed evangelism. There they'd be, waiting and ready for the conference attendees to exit their meeting and trudge bravely through the crowded public spaces that now resembled a bizarro religious version of the New York Stock Exchange on a history-making day.

I like to think of this arrangement between Latter-day Saints and their protesters as a preview to what social media would ultimately become: strangers yelling non sequiturs at one another while trying to crowd the space with their own opinion in an effort to drown out anything else. Maybe it was impossible for a religion founded during the Second Great Awakening to avoid this chaotic, contentious and raucous fate.

I lived in an apartment near Temple Square in my late 20s. This was after I stopped going to church. I always knew when General Conference weekend had arrived, not only because of the obvious increase in minivan traffic, but also because the bagpipes, shouts and strained singing filled the atmosphere on Saturday morning and didn't let up until at least dinnertime on Sunday.

I confess I haven't conducted any real investigation on this, nor have I ever seen any data. But I've always assumed no one surrounding Temple Square on General Conference weekend is engaging in any sort of effective missionary work. I could certainly be wrong about that. Maybe the bearded brigade has plucked away a Latter-day Saint who was on the fence about whether fire and brimstone are really all that bad. Or maybe the white shirts and ties holding up copies of the Book of Mormon and declaring it true has changed someone's mind about whether there should be an expensive private reflection pond on Main Street.

It sounds like I'm being glib, and I probably mostly am, but I do really wonder about all this effort we put into yelling at one another. If it doesn't change hearts and minds, isn't it a waste of energy and well-being? I once heard that advocacy without a sincere attempt to persuade only serves the activist. Is the yelling motivated by a sincere attempt to persuade? Maybe. Maybe the screamers and singers really believe their efforts might amount to a successful recruitment.

Or it might be the case that everyone is down there in our state's capital a couple of times a year damning one another to hell simply because they find it fun. I doubt that's true. Or at least, I hope it's not true, because that somehow makes it all more depressing.

The old Main Street/now plaza is currently under reconstruction, along with much of the rest of Temple Square and the surrounding church properties. I don't know what the plaza will look like in its next aesthetic iteration, but I assume the rules will continue to forbid protesting there. And I assume that won't stop the protesters and counter protesters from filling public sidewalks in the surrounding areas. No, the great and loud biannual missionary war will continue in some form.

Maybe there will come a day when religion doesn't require anyone to actively recruit those who don't want to be recruited, a day when people are entitled to peacefully live their beliefs with sufficient confidence that their example is evangelism enough. Maybe the bagpipes will get mysteriously and irreparably punctured.

Until then, I'll be here in my house, trying my darndest to avoid the free hugs.

# Temple Marriage

My first date with my now husband, Skylar, was at the Kirtland Temple in Ohio. This wasn't intentional.

I had connected with him on a dating app because he had touched down at the Salt Lake City International Airport for a one-hour layover. He was living in Wisconsin at the time, and when I discovered this, I figured there was no way we'd ever actually meet each other. Then, after a month of talking on the phone for several hours every day, he called me up and invited me to be his plus-one at a wedding in Cleveland.

A friend took me to the airport for my red-eye flight a few weeks later. During the drive, I told her I was going to arrive in Cleveland some 12 hours before Skylar, I couldn't check into my hotel room until the afternoon, and I didn't know how I was going to kill some time after I landed. That's when she informed me Kirtland is only 20 or so minutes outside of Cleveland.

Having grown up a Latter-day Saint, I was, of course, familiar with the stories of my pioneer ancestors' sojourn in Kirtland. Families in my neighborhood in the '90s—the kind who all wore matching BYU T-shirts and went to church on vacation—would even plan entire family pilgrimages to the place every few summers.

I had stopped going to church a year or two before, so it was perhaps an odd thing that the next morning I found myself on an extended one-on-one tour of the Kirtland Temple led by an elderly man sporting a wizarding beard that ran down to his navel. I guess it seemed to me it would have been a shame to not pop by this place that had occupied hundreds of Sunday school conversations from my childhood, given that I was staying just one town over.

I don't know how long the tour lasted, but it felt like hours. The tour guide told me that since the place was empty, he had time to give me an extended lecture about the building and its history, which he then did without breaking eye contact for the better part of the morning.

As we descended the stairs at the conclusion of the presentation, he asked me if I was musically inclined. I thought he was just making small talk. I didn't know at the time that the tour of the Kirtland Temple traditionally ends with the tour group convening in the main chapel area of the building to sing a vibrant rendition of a classic Mormon hymn, "The Spirit of God." Had I known this, I probably wouldn't have volunteered that I sometimes dabbled in the piano in response to his question.

The next thing I knew, I found myself accompanying my tour guide as he belted all hundred or so verses of the hymn, his right hand resting on the piano, foot a-tapping, and openly weeping down his long white beard. It was sometime during this musical performance when it occurred to me that my attempt to fly to Ohio to go on a gay date with a man I had found on the internet had already gone very off the rails in the most surprising way possible.

When Skylar arrived in Cleveland late that evening, we briefly met in the hotel lobby, where he asked me what I had been up to all day. I word-vomited the story at him, watching a look of confusion and concern cloud his face as I blurted out words like "temple" and "missionary" and "altar" and "everlasting covenants."

Skylar did not grow up religious and had no exposure to Mormonism, and as I heard myself recounting the experience, it occurred to me I probably sounded to him like a religious fanatic, and I wouldn't have been surprised if he had started glancing around for the exits. But just before I had an opportunity to acknowledge how strange this all surely seemed, he leaned in and asked in amazement, "Would you be willing to go back there tomorrow?"

The next morning, we drove 20 minutes to take a romantic tour of the Kirtland Temple. I couldn't help but stand in awe that what might have scared away many others seemed instead to be a bonding experience for us. I was touched, in fact, by his fascination and his sincere attempt to understand and appreciate this part of my background as we stood in front of a desk the tour guide explained to us was used by church founder Joseph Smith himself. (Skylar supportively gasped and put one hand to his chest when this fact was shared, even though he didn't know who Joseph Smith was.)

There were other visitors when we arrived: a large family wearing matching BYU T-shirts. The mother was aggressive in volunteering to play the piano, and her children sounded like The Tabernacle Choir at Temple Square.

We left Kirtland at the end of the morning, giggling, well aware how odd of a first date this was. I was still half convinced once the weekend was over that I would never hear from Skylar again. But he continued to surprise me by not ghosting me. Instead, he moved to Salt Lake City many months later, and we got engaged not long after that.

While growing up, I was told that one day I'd get married in a temple. That, of course, didn't happen. But it seems only fair to give half credit to the church leaders of my youth considering that I did fall in love in one.

# Skobetang

In 2012, I accepted a job as legal counsel for the judiciary in Palau, a small island nation in the equatorial Pacific. I had graduated from law school the year before and the legal job market was still in the toilet after the 2008 financial crisis. So, even though I had never even heard of Palau, let alone set foot in that part of the world, I was ecstatic to have a (very low-paying) job in the tropics.

The entire population of Palau is fewer than 20,000 people, and they are spread over eight islands. The island where my apartment sat was about 1 square mile in size. It was connected by a long causeway to the island where my office was—the most populated island, barely larger than the one where I lived.

On my first Sunday in Palau, I discovered there was a small congregation, called a branch, of The Church of Jesus Christ of Latter-day Saints in the country. This period of my life was near the end of my church activity, but I was still a Bible-thumper, so I was thrilled to find out there were fellow members in town, and I dutifully showed up in my Sunday best for the 11 a.m. service.

Minutes after I walked into the small plain building where we would have sacrament meeting, an 8-year-old Palauan boy asked if I was a lawyer. I said yes and asked how he guessed. He looked down at my feet and said, "Because you're wearing shoes." I would spend the next 12 months exclusively wearing sandals like everyone else, doing my best to blend in.

A week later, I was asked to serve as Young Men president for the seven teenage boys who came to church. Before my arrival, the exhausted branch president had been filling this spot as well as several others. I was 28 years old and felt unequipped, but I agreed to do it.

Palau is the most beautiful place I've ever been. The hundreds of thick jungled islands are surrounded by miles of vibrant coral reef and water the temperature of a comfortable bath. Every morning,

I'd step onto the balcony of my apartment and look over a bay below and wonder how this place could possibly be real. And yet, this was a hard year for me.

The isolation of small-town living on a relatively inaccessible island with spotty and expensive internet access and almost no air conditioning was new to me. I was also a terrified closeted gay man and struggling with what I now realize was a painful faith crisis, thousands of miles away from family and friends, who were all living their lives on the opposite side of the world. To put it mildly, I was severely depressed.

Considering some of that, it might surprise people to hear that serving as Young Men president was perhaps the most grounding and comforting aspect of my life at that time. Because the branch was small and many callings were not filled, we usually combined the Young Women and Young Men groups for activities and classes. I would spend hours every week with these teens, who were hilarious and kind and entertaining in all the ways teens all over the world can be.

I referred to them as "the church kids" to my non-Latter-day-Saint co-workers and friends, who found it charming that I often couldn't drive my white beat-up Suzuki anywhere on the islands without being flagged down by one of them for a ride, or just to tag along on my errand. They would come to my apartment for help with their homework or mission papers or, in some sad cases, to talk about their struggles at home.

My job was on a 12-month contract, so, after a year, I packed up my apartment and began my farewell tour. I cried saying goodbye to the friends I had made, but none of the goodbyes were as hard to deliver as those I said to the church kids. Not long before I left the islands, the church kids gave me a Palauan nickname, "Skobetang," which I was told means "shotgun." I have no idea why this was the name they picked, but I chose not to ask too many questions and to instead just be touched.

I think of that experience serving as Young Men leader as my Mormonism grand finale—my great send-off into my life of hooliganism and, you know, buckets full of sin and wickedness. And I feel really lucky that's the way I got to go out.

It's funny to look back on, now. I wasn't living many of the church rules and standards while serving as Young Men president. I mean, I fully had a live-in boyfriend and even drank wine on at least one occasion. And yet, there I was every Sunday morning in a shirt, tie and sandals, talking to a church youth group about Jesus, and helping those who were interested prepare to serve missions. (I sent two missionaries off during that year.)

Some people might call that duplicitous or hypocritical or some other word that describes incongruent living. I have no appetite or reason to argue against any of that. Cognitive dissonance and faith exoduses are a hell of a thing, and I'm not sure anyone who hasn't gone through the latter can really understand what that feels like.

Still, there's no part of me that regrets any of it. My life may have been messy, but I was there for those kids and they were there for me, and that will always be one of my great life joys and proudest achievements.

I married six years later, in 2019, and my husband, Skylar, and I decided to honeymoon in Palau. This was my first time returning to the islands, which were even more beautiful and vibrant than I had remembered.

I hadn't been to church in more than half a decade and had no intention of ever going back, but I couldn't resist bringing Skylar to visit that little Palauan branch.

There was a small part of me that felt nervous to parade in my gay husband and introduce him to these Latter-day Saint congregants who had entrusted their children's spiritual well-being with me years earlier. Yet, somehow I knew if ever there was a Latter-day Saint congregation that would be cool about this, this was the one.

We were welcomed with open arms. The church kids, most of them adults by then, updated me on their studies and, in some cases, showed off their spouses. The branch president, the same one who asked me to lead the Young Men, invited me to tell everyone what I was now doing in my life. I introduced Skylar and explained this was our honeymoon, and the branch embraced him every bit as much as those members embraced me.

After the service, I stood at the corner of the room with one of the church kids, Skarlee, who was then 24.

"I hope it wasn't too big of a surprise for everyone," I said, "to find out I'm gay and married to a man now."

Skarlee laughed. "Everyone always knew you were gay," he responded.

"Really?" I asked, as if I had been caught.

"Oh, Skobetang," he said. "We were all just hoping you would one day be happy."

# The Pioneers Wouldn't Trade Us Places

"Yes, the pioneers had it hard. But if they could see the temptations and trials of today, they wouldn't trade us places."

It was my then-85-year-old grandma who said it over a plate of Mormon comfort foods—mashed potatoes that had been underbeaten by a fork, a side of brown roast and an even browner mound of what I assume were once vegetables.

Everyone around the dinner table politely nodded. An hour later, I climbed into the car with my then-boyfriend (now husband). The moment he shut the passenger door, he asked me about it.

"What was that pioneer thing all about?"

I often forget he didn't come from a Mormon family in the heart of Zion like I did, and so sentiments that often roll over me (a person who grew up with pictures of Jesus hanging in the bathrooms) sound like alien proclamations to him. His cultural inquiries had already become commonplace by the time he heard my grandma's pioneer remark. Only weeks before this, a family member said she felt the presence of the Holy Ghost and he, in absolute sincerity, whispered, "How spooky!"

We once came across a statue of the resurrected Lord hovering over Mary and he whispered into my ear, "Is that supposed to be David Blaine?"

One time he asked me what Mormon missionaries do all day, so I told him they talk to people who are "investigating" the church. He gasped, put one hand to his chest, and asked, "Like the FBI?"

It doesn't come from a place of mockery, truly. They're wholly innocent, his observations. Many of them sound as generous as others sound critical. Not long ago he overheard a passing reference to "the woman taken in adultery" so he asked what that meant. I shared the story—about how Jesus told the judgmental scribes and Pharisees to pound sand. When I finished the summary, my teary-eyed husband responded, "Awe. Jesus seems like he was a really sweet guy."

So I wasn't surprised that he had never heard this saying about Mormon pioneers and our hypothetical pissing match with them over the generational size of our respective trials and tribulations. Nor did it catch me off guard that he would have found my grandma's declaration unusual.

"It's something I've heard throughout my life," I explained to him. "People often say the pioneers wouldn't trade us places because our challenges today are so overwhelming."

He wasn't buying it, and he asked me to give him an example of a temptation from the modern world that would so terrify the pioneers that they'd give up access to TV just to avoid it.

"Well," I said, "some people think the pioneers would be horrified with internet pornography."

He was quiet for a moment, and then he pushed back.

"I'm pretty sure if I told the pioneers I could give them consistent access to hot water that comes out of a faucet in their climate-controlled home with down pillows in every room and a washer and dryer in the basement, and in exchange they just had to avoid looking at naked people through a piece of glass, I'd have some takers."

In the years since my grandma spoke this cultural aphorism, he has referenced the pioneer "lie" as often as he could find an opening.

"Could you imagine going to the dentist in the 19th century to have a tooth pulled without proper pain medication?" a friend once said to us.

"Yes," my sarcastic husband responded. "But if the pioneers could see what we go through today, they wouldn't trade us places. Do you really think they'd want modern medicine if it meant they also had to deal with navigating Costco crowds on a Saturday?"

I can't stop him at this point, and I'm not sure I want to. I left The Church of Jesus Christ of Latter-day Saints and haven't been religious in nearly a decade. Naturally, I have a lot of complicated feelings about my former religion, so these takedowns of my youth's adages sometimes feel like a high-five—validating, if not satisfying. But then he'll see my Mormon mother write in his birthday card "I'm so glad to have you in our forever family" and he'll say to me, "What a nice concept—that you should try to love your family so much that you want to be with them forever." As much as I'd sometimes like to pretend otherwise, I can't deny those moments often bring tears to my eyes.

Recently we went camping. I don't know why. We aren't any good at it. We spent hours chopping wood with a dull ax, starting a pitiful fire, and cooking bland food over smoldering coals. We eventually climbed into our tent to lie on rocky ground that somehow seemed to be equally sloped in every possible direction. I, shivering, snuggled over to my husband to try to find some warmth.

"This is miserable," I murmured.

"So miserable," he groaned.

Then I heard a quiet giggle before he continued.

"I bet the pioneers wouldn't trade us places."

# The Cookie Situation

Not long ago, one of my sisters got married. My parents were very involved in the wedding preparations, which is how we ended up in what my family now refers to as "The Cookie Situation."

"You need to come see this," one of my siblings told me as the reception wrapped up. "You won't believe me unless you see it for yourself."

We walked to the venue's kitchen area, where nearly 20 large boxes of massive frosted cookies sat unopened and untouched. "There must be hundreds of cookies here," this sister said before launching into a triage to try to figure out what to do with all the leftover food.

We later did the calculation. My sweet parents had ordered enough cookies for each anticipated guest to have half a dozen. "I don't know why we thought that was an appropriate amount," my mother said, shaking her head. "I don't know why we ordered so many."

I knew why.

My mother, like her parents before her, and their parents before them, back to Mormon pioneer days, were raised this way. The same way I was raised—to feed. To overfeed. We were brought up to prepare food not for what will be, but for what could be. To embody the physical manifestation of Jesus' miracle with the loaves and fishes. To call upon our most gluttonously animalistic impulses conceived during Mormonism's inaugural breaths.

To descend from Mormonism is to fear running out of food more than to fear waste.

When my mother became aware of The Cookie Situation, she grabbed one of the boxes and trudged out to the street, begging strangers to take them. "Please," I heard her beseech a passerby. "We have too many cookies, and we just don't know what to do."

The next morning my husband drove his Subaru around the valley dropping off the remaining unsolicited boxes at shelters and children's hospitals. When he returned home, he shook his head. "I will never understand this part of your family."

He has tried to train these same impulses out of me but in the nine years I've known him, he hasn't made any progress.

"Now remember," he said to me last July as I started preparing a potato salad for a four-person picnic, "a very small bowl will be more than sufficient."

"Right," I sincerely told him, determined to self-moderate.

The moment he left the kitchen I experienced a possession not even the most seasoned exorcist could have restrained. The spirits of my ancestors entered my body and used my hands to peel 20 pounds of potatoes and boil a dozen eggs. I have not even a whiff of a memory of any of this. I remember only the outcome.

"I don't know what happened," I told my husband as we stood over our two largest bowls, each heaped with enough bland potato salad to feed 20 families at a potluck in a Pleasant Grove meetinghouse.

He sighed.

I know I've always been this way, but I don't think I understood there was something wrong with me until I visited my husband's family in Washington for the first time and attended a dinner at his sister's house.

"How is such an offering meant to feed this many people?" I whispered to my husband as his sister pulled from the oven a sparse roasting pan of 12 asparagus spears and presented them to the 15 people in attendance.

"May the Lord sustain us in the coming months after suffering this season's destitute harvest," I mumbled in despair upon surveying the platter of five divided chicken breasts. (Note: I implicitly start speaking like a 19th-century God-fearing farmer down on his luck whenever I worry there isn't going to be enough food at any given event.)

"Not everyone will want asparagus, so this was an appropriate amount to make," my husband explained, as though conservative predictions about realistic food consumption should be a routine part of planning meals.

The family members sat around the table, politely portioning out reasonable amounts of the various dishes until none was left. They ate. They then stood up and cleaned the empty modest receptacles. No waste. No leftovers. I believe leftovers were never anticipated. I don't think this kitchen even had a Tupperware drawer filled with empty Cool Whip containers from the '90s.

There must be a reason so many of us in Utah know only how to cook for 20. Maybe it's because, unlike many other families, ours haven't historically chugged wine with dinner, so we turned to an overindulgence in food as our vice of choice. Maybe this behavior is the result of residual cultural trauma from our ancestors' brutal pioneer treks across the plains. Maybe there's a little genetic part of us that still thinks we all belong to large polygamous families. Maybe it's a dash of all those things.

But even if genetics can contribute, I did recently learn environmental factors may be just as culpable a cause in some.

A few months ago, my husband and I hosted a small neighborhood gathering in our backyard. He ordered a number of large pizzas from a place down the street and assigned me to get them as he put the final touches on the several gallons of sangria he had just made a mess in our kitchen preparing.

When I gave the establishment my husband's name, the workers directed me to eight large pizza boxes, each with 10 slices. "Are you sure you have the right order?" I asked, doing basic math in my head and determining this would be enough pizza for nearly each attendee to have a box.

The order was confirmed, and I returned home with the 80 slices of pizza to feed our 10 neighbors.

At night's end, my husband and I stood over six untouched boxes of leftover pizza and six wine bottles' worth of sangria. "I don't know why I thought this was an appropriate amount of food," my husband said, in disbelief. "I don't even remember ordering or making this much."

I put my arm around him, squeezed his shoulder and whispered, "Welcome to Zion."

He looked at me, wide-eyed and concerned as I whispered

again, smiling and staring at him like a hypnotic predator who finally captured its prey.

"We've been waiting for you to join us."

# Custom-Fit Tuxedo

I came out to my parents in their kitchen one Saturday morning when I was 29. The night before, a gay friend gave me some advice for the conversation. "Don't beat around the bush," he said. "Just come out with it. And be unequivocal. Don't leave room for doubt because that might cause confusion."

My dad was reading a newspaper, and my mom was slouched over her sewing machine working on a project for her highly competitive quilting group.

"I have something to tell you," I began. "I am incredibly gay."

My dad put down his newspaper and frowned in confusion. My mother eyed me over her glasses that were down at the end of her nose.

"Is incredibly gay different from regular gay?" she asked.

Once I clarified that, no, I didn't think the amplifier really made a difference, that I was just trying to be unequivocal, they settled into the news with relative ease.

This was 2014. I was aware the conversation with them went much differently than it might have 10 or 15 years earlier. I had been inundated throughout my religious childhood with church messaging about the evil homosexuals who lurked among us. In the 1990s, Sunday school teachers regularly told me "one of Satan's tactics is to convince people they are born gay, but we know that's not true. People choose to be gay, and that is a sin."

I wasn't sure, at age 12, when exactly I had "chosen" to have a crush on every boy in middle school (and I mean all of them). I figured this was maybe one of those opt-in things when you enter a raffle in which you also accidentally sign up to receive an eternal onslaught of marketing materials. Or maybe it happened when I saw *Titanic* and Leonardo DiCaprio broke my brain.

In any event, I knew, based on how we all talked about the

wicked gays, it would not be a good idea for me to acknowledge doodling Jonathan Taylor Thomas' name in my notebook during English class. (The one that got away.)

The change in our religious community wasn't quick, but I started to notice movement over the next 10 years. As a young adult, I heard Larry King ask Gordon B. Hinckley, then-president of The Church of Jesus Christ of Latter-day Saints, whether he believed people were born gay. To my surprise at the time, Hinckley said he didn't know the answer to that. It seemed shortly after this interview that the "nobody is born gay" rhetoric died away.

A few years later, the church tried to put every shoulder to the wheel on California's Proposition 8. "I was pressured to stand on the side of a road with a sign," a friend said to me recently. "It was so embarrassing. Now I donate regularly to the Human Rights Campaign like I'm paying a fine."

I told her not to be too hard on herself. We're all paying penance in our own ways for past regressive actions and beliefs we feel guilty about now. When I was 8, my mother and I were riding our bikes back from Blockbuster and she crashed into a curb. As blood gushed from her chin, I had the gall to shout, "Are the videos okay?" Whenever this memory pops into my head, I go to the internet to order her flowers.

After Prop 8, there seemed to be a number of shifts in a more gentle direction. There were steps backward and forward, to be sure, but mostly people were warming up to us. The church even supported some policy initiatives that would provide protection to LGBTQ individuals.

So, yes, by the time I came out to my parents, we were living in a much different world than the one from when I was 12. Still, I would be ungrateful not to acknowledge that they did always seem at least a few steps ahead of most people in their community on this issue. I always knew they would support me. So it wasn't a surprise when my mother ran a piece of fabric through her sewing machine and shouted over its aggressive hum, "Now that you've told us, I hope you can relax and find some peace. We love you, honey."

A few years later, they each gave teary speeches at my wedding when I married my husband, Skylar. Skylar is a physician, and several months ago my mom had major surgery to remove some invasive cancer, so, in an attempt to be helpful, he went with her to every doctor appointment and sat with her and my dad for hours on end while she recovered. One night I went to visit her in the hospital and a nurse told me out in the hallway my mom had bragged to every hospital staffer she had seen that her son-in-law "is a doctor."

As I sat with her next to her bed, she turned to me, with weepy eyes, and said, "Skylar is a very good man. You married a very good man."

This was never the future I imagined for myself when I was 12. And not just because I didn't end up with Jonathan Taylor Thomas. But it's the reality that somehow came to be in Utah, a state where the population now overwhelmingly believes same-sex marriage should be legal. Even my former church recently expressed support for the newly enacted Respect for Marriage Act, which codifies some currently recognized constitutional protections. Who could have predicted this shift?

Somehow, in just two decades, I went from living in a world where I never thought I could come out, to one where my parents call my husband more than they call me. That's so lovely that I often forget to be offended about it.

About three months before our wedding, my husband and I spent an evening measuring our sassy poodle mix so we could order him a custom tux from a high-end boutique pet clothing designer in London.

"We need to make sure his color scheme matches the table centerpieces I just bought," Skylar said to me.

As we typed out a long email detailing our very particular requests, the dog at that moment wearing a bow tie and sitting on a silk pillow near our feet, I couldn't help but chuckle at how over-the-top it all was.

We waited far too long to legalize this.

# Resigned

When I stopped attending my Latter-day Saint ward in 2014, I never really had any intention of going through the formal process of coordinating with corporate to cancel my relationship with God. Having my church membership records removed seemed like a pain, and I wasn't particularly motivated to do this.

There was a time when I would fantasize about being excommunicated in a tribunal of neighborhood volunteer dads. I had a speech prepared and everything. The vision involved at least two members of my jury being moved to tears and walking out with me. But it turned out I wasn't interesting or important enough to prosecute for my hooliganism, so instead of being hunted down for persecution, I was sought out for reactivation.

At one point I had moved to a new neighborhood, and my membership records somehow followed me. One Sunday afternoon, two timid men knocked on my front door to invite me to start attending the ward. I politely declined. (It has always been my personal policy to never be rude to the door knockers in these situations because I remember what it was like to be on the other side of the exchange.)

A week later, I received a card in the mail from one of those men, notifying me that he had informed the other congregation members I wasn't interested in contact. He concluded the note, "Please know I'm not just a member of the ward. I'm also your neighbor, if you ever need one. I hope you'll consider this sincere fellowship." I never did contact him, but it's been 11 years, and I confess I still have that card.

Eventually whoever is in charge of this sort of thing (Moses?) transferred my membership records to my parents' ward. I discovered this when I began receiving an onslaught of emails from the ward activities committee, elders quorum, and whatever poor soul had been assigned to beg people to clean meetinghouse toilets every Saturday. I responded to these emails, asking to be removed from the list. Nevertheless, the emails continued. I wasn't too annoyed with this because, again, I had been on the other side of this type of outreach, and I knew what I was experiencing was probably more a matter of disorganization than targeted harassment.

My attitude about all this finally changed after several years of receiving these emails when one evening a new bishop, whom I did not know, sent out a ward newsletter praising the family proclamation as divinely inspired. By this time, I was happily married to my husband, wondering why, after years of requesting to be left alone, I was being sent propaganda that denounced my family.

In a moment I now recognize as rage, I hit reply to the email and typed, "I have been asking to be taken off this list for years. Do I have to have my church membership records removed to get you people to leave me alone?"

I wrote other things as well, but the absolute tyrants who published this won't let me swear so I can't share the rest of it here. The point is, it was the most impolite email I had ever sent, and for that I would like to publicly apologize to my mother who raised me to leave five-star customer reviews even when the experience was bad because "we don't know what kind of day that man was having so let's not make it worse."

The bishop responded quickly, apologizing, and explaining he wasn't aware of my prior requests. He promised there would be no contact going forward and offered to assist with my record removal, if I wanted, by either having me send him a notarized letter or by meeting with him to sign a letter in his presence.

Once my temper subsided, I debated ardently with myself about whether I cared enough about this to go through the steps. And thus began a two-year period wherein I delivered a daily monologue to my husband, who had never been religious and whose eyes would glaze over as I spoke because he could not possibly understand why I was treating any of this as more momentous than canceling a Netflix subscription.

The monologue: "Maybe I should just remove my records. Sometimes the church does things I find morally offensive, and I don't want to be counted among their ranks. And by having my records removed, I would be informing them I don't approve. Or would that communicate that I think it matters whether they consider me a member? Maybe that would be a way of giving them power over me. Also, having my records removed might make my parents sad. Or maybe my parents don't care at all, and I'm overthinking it. Or am I underthinking it? Should I go back to therapy?"

My husband would then yell "yes" to that last question and change the subject.

I eventually became exhausted with having this weigh on me, so one evening I reached out to this bishop and asked if I could come by and get this over with. I informed my parents and they were supportive and wished me luck, confirming that I had overthought at least some of this.

A few days later, I knocked on this bishop's door. He was friendly, if not a little nervous, and he invited me into his living room, plastered with pictures of temples. We engaged in several minutes of small talk.

"Your parents sure are great."

"Yes, they sure are great."

"They're the backbone of the ward."

"They're the backbone of my family." Etc.

It felt like a parent-teacher conference.

After 20 minutes, I had the old urge to pull out an *Ensign* magazine and share a home teaching message, but it was at this point the bishop handed me a laptop so I could write my resignation letter.

As I placed my hands on the keyboard, it suddenly occurred to me I had no idea what this letter was supposed to say. I asked for help, but he confessed he also didn't know. It was then that this poor bishop began Googling anti-Mormon websites for instructions on how to resign from The Church of Jesus Christ of Latter-day Saints.

I hope they're paying him enough.

While he did some research, I decided to take a crack at it, and, to my surprise, the most formal 19th-century religious language buried deep down began pouring out of me, and I found myself typing something like "Dear The Church, I hereby forevermore relinquish unto you my everlasting covenants, in the name of the Father, the Son, and the Holy Ghost."

I showed the bishop my draft and asked if what I had written would work. He looked at it, puzzled, and then muttered, "I think they'll get the point."

A moment later, the letter was printed, and the bishop handed it and a pen to me. Sitting on his couch, I asked if he had a book or something I could use for the signing. Habitually, he reached for something on a side table, and I noticed he froze. I looked over and saw that he had begun to grab the largest copy of the Book of Mormon I had ever seen, before realizing it might not be appropriate to use that as the desk for my resignation.

We looked at each other, and he appeared ready to apologize.

The irony then hit me. Here was the book that started it all. The book that caused my pioneer ancestors to trek. The book that raised me. The book that led my dad to take my 8-year-old hand and guide me into a baptismal font. The book that sent me to Ukraine for two years. The book that had caused me anguish, the same anguish that finally led me out of the closet and to a new identity, separate from this religious life that had guided every part of who I had been. And this was now the book this bishop nearly gave me to formalize my rejection of what I felt had already rejected me.

It all seemed so poetic, and hilarious in a way, and suddenly I smiled at him, pointed to the book, and said, somewhat bluntly, "Well, actually, that's perfect."

The bishop smirked and handed me the book. I began to sign just as I started to laugh. He started laughing as well. In the next room, I could hear snickers from his family members, who no doubt had been briefed on our awkward meeting and could probably hear every word of it. And the laughing from everyone only amused me more, to the point that my shaky signature looked nothing like my own.

I handed the letter to the bishop. He walked me to the door and wished me well. As I shook his hand, it occurred to me my experience of leaving the church was consistent with most of my key experiences with Mormonism: painful and conflicted, sometimes confusing, but nonetheless surrounded by a community I love, often despite itself.

My grand exit didn't include a speech or a juicy tribunal. And it certainly didn't prompt any tears—but instead, laughter.

In short, it was perfect.

# And That's When I Knew

My dating days were frequently filled with angst, a type not uncommon for many people. I was often frozen in decision-making fear.

I knew I wanted to marry one day, I guess because I hoped to have someone live in my house and judge me for how much TV I watch. But I wasn't sure how I was supposed to know when I found "the one." I would ask married friends how they acquired sufficient confidence their now spouse was the right person. They'd tell me stories—an experience that gave them some clarity. They saw their partner interact well with children. Or they witnessed a kind act or a selfless gesture. Maybe they found out their significant other was rich.

Each of these stories had something in common. They'd all end with the storyteller saying some variation of "and that's when I knew."

I figured I couldn't marry someone until I had a moment with the person I could one day identify as the very instant I realized we were destined to be. I can see now I was putting too much pressure on myself and creating unreasonable rules for my dates, often to my own detriment. If enough time passed without a moment of enlightenment, I'd get antsy and move on, even if I liked my dates and was having a nice time getting to know them.

It took far too long to shed this expectation, but with a lot of work and some fatigue, I finally chilled out. I was going to date and stay with the same person for as long as it was interesting and enjoyable. And if we ultimately decided to marry, well, even better. I would no longer stress over finding my "and that's when I knew" moment.

It was around this time I met my now husband, Skylar. He was living in Wisconsin and I in Salt Lake City. The long-distance relationship was not ideal, but we traveled to visit one another as often as we could and had a great time together. Before long, it became obvious that we'd never really get to know each other well enough, or perhaps build a life together, if we were living a thousand miles apart. No, one of us would have to move, and I did not want to be that person because I had too much stuff. Also, Wisconsin is cold.

To say I essentially became an overeager, rose-colored real estate agent for Utah over the next several months is an understatement. I devoted substantial time and energy trying to woo Skylar to the Beehive State like I was attempting to score a selection from the International Olympic Committee. Every time he visited, I'd take him on a whirlwind tour of our best sites. We explored the resorts. We hiked the canyons. I made sure to point out frequently how short the drive was—"when you think about it"—to each of our national parks.

Skylar quickly began to fall in love with Salt Lake City. As he started to contemplate relocating, I figured it would probably constitute Deseret recruiting fraud, or at least malpractice, not to educate him on the sometimes-complicated nature of living as a gay person side by side with this state's predominant religion. I decided for his next visit I'd need to take him on a tour of Temple Square and explain some things.

My intention was always to give him a neutral, almost bland anthropological presentation and introduction to Mormonism. He had no history with it so there was no reason to hand him any of my baggage.

I planned to walk him around the grounds to see the beautiful architecture. I'd tell him about my pioneer history and how my ancestors helped break ground for the temple. I'd help him generally understand the church's less-than-commendable history on LGBTQ issues. We'd admire the landscaping. And we'd finish the excursion by attending the Tabernacle Choir's live Sunday morning broadcast, *Music and the Spoken Word.*

I expected he'd enjoy that last part—that it might leave a good enough taste in his mouth so that some of the other stuff wouldn't scare him away. You don't have to be religious to be impressed with the vocal abilities of this world-renowned musical body, propped in front of a famous and imposing 19th-century organ inside a domed religious edifice that serves as living proof of pioneer architectural ingenuity.

We entered the Tabernacle that morning and took our seats on the south balcony. Moments later, the 300-plus singers entered, the women clad in matching muumuus and the men wearing matching suits. Some warmups were conducted and, after a few minutes, overhead cameras glided across the room as announcer Lloyd Newell took to the podium to begin the televised broadcast and welcome the audience who would then sit and listen to 30 minutes of religious caroling.

The performance was flawless, as I expected. The choir, in fact, sounded better than I remembered. It was like the singers were all secret allies, and they knew I had brought a man there I was trying to impress. I was pleased this was going so well.

I was excited to hear what Skylar thought. I expected he was captivated, mostly because he sat in critical silence throughout the performance. I planned to ask him for his thoughts on our drive home, but as the choir began singing the last number, "God Be with You till We Meet Again," he leaned ever so slightly toward me to whisper something, signaling, perhaps, that he was eager to give me his reaction.

"Wow," he said. I glanced at him and nodded my head as if to respond, "I know, right?"

Then he continued his review.

"Incredible," he whispered. Pointing toward the choir members in their matching robes, he shook his head in amazement and then mumbled into my ear, "What are the chances they'd all show up wearing the same outfit?"

It took a moment or two for his bad joke to sink in, but sink in it did. There, amid a teary-eyed congregation that was being actively moved by the broadcast, all he could do was find amusement.

And I just sat there, thinking, in exasperation and calling upon some dormant prudish impulses buried deep within my formerly religious soul, "Where is his reverence? This sarcastic smart aleck doesn't take anything seriously. He is willing to make a joke out of anything."

I abruptly turned and looked at him, these thoughts running

through my mind. He was smiling, proud of himself and clearly wanting credit for being funny. There was a twinkle in his sarcastic eyes, and I immediately realized a life with him would include very few moments of somber solemness.

And that's when I knew.

# Cousins by the Dozens

My parents come from Mormon pioneer stock, which means my second cousins outnumber the sands of the sea.

If you're from Utah, there's a good chance you and I have been invited to several of the same family reunions. I once did one of those Ancestry DNA tests and when the software attempted to populate my family tree, it crashed the system and caused power outages in nine counties.

There's a scene in *My Big Fat Greek Wedding* in which the protagonist is explaining to her WASPy new boyfriend that her family is different—that meeting all of them might be overwhelming. "I have 27 first cousins," she emphasizes. "Just 27 first cousins alone."

I saw this film in 2002. I was 17. I thought the point she was trying to make was that she had a small family, and that's why they were all constantly up in one another's business. I thought that because, by that time, I already had somewhere around 70 first cousins, and I thought that was normal.

When my Portland-born hippie husband moved to Salt Lake City, and I tried to explain this to him, he thought I was confused. "No," he said. "You must be counting second and third cousins, plus the once-removeds and close family friends. No one has that many first cousins."

I had to draw a diagram to explain how it was possible for my mother's nine siblings and my father's seven siblings to produce enough children to fill out the roster for an entire Division 1 college football team.

Even after he seemed to understand this on paper, the implications of having such a deep family bench never fully sank in. This became obvious several years ago when we received a mailed wedding invitation from one of my youngest cousins who had met her fiancé the previous week and was marrying him the following week.

"Such short notice!" my panicking husband shouted. "Thank God we're in town! Did this invitation get lost in the mail for a year?" Then he turned over the simple card several times. "Hmm. I don't see a way to RSVP."

We had just spent the summer traveling to America's most inconvenient destinations to participate in a nearly never-ending stream of wedding ceremonies for his college friends who had devoted more time and energy to planning their festivities than the International Olympic Committee does in executing a global event. I realized, based on his reaction to my cousin's announcement, I had never braced him for the often comparatively chaotic simplicity of a slapdash Utah Latter-day Saint wedding.

I tried to explain we weren't invited to the wedding itself. That would be a small religious ceremony we'd have to engage in substantial life changes to even be allowed to witness. We were just being welcomed to swing by one evening to a Latter-day Saint meetinghouse, where streamers might dangle from basketball hoops and children we are somehow related to would be running wildly through carpet-walled hallways wearing clip-on ties and their most recent grass-stained Easter dresses.

Nevertheless, he entered the reception into our shared iPhone calendar and ordered the couple a gift from their Target registry.

The following week, he texted me while I was still at work to ask what time I thought we should leave for the open house. This was a Thursday, and I just then realized I had scheduled a conflicting evening appointment. I called him and explained I didn't think we'd be able to make it to the reception. In his most concerned tone, he told me we couldn't just not show up to celebrate these family nuptials, no doubt picturing the opening scene of *The Godfather* and imagining a disappointed, powerful, raspy-voiced uncle upset that we flaked out "on the day my daughter is to be married."

I tried to explain, again, that there really was no expectation that we actually attend. "They sent out hundreds of these, like a house flipper spamming mailboxes with offers to buy homes for cash in the neighborhood. Besides, I barely know this cousin. I'm pretty sure we wouldn't even recognize each other in a crowd."

"Oh, that can't be true," he argued. "I can't imagine someone not knowing their first cousin who lives mere miles from them unless there was family drama that would have kept them apart."

"No family drama," I clarified. "But I'm telling you, this is not a close relationship."

"I doubt they see it that way," he said.

"They misspelled both our names on the envelope," I reminded him, "and misgendered you."

He waved me away and said if I couldn't make it, he'd at least go by himself "to represent our family."

I wished him luck.

He arrived home that evening around 9:30, looking bewildered.

"How was it?" I asked.

"There were so many people there and no program or any organization to it at all," he said. "Also, they didn't really have any food."

I chuckled. "Just butter mints and half-frozen eclairs?"

He looked surprised, like he just discovered he might be married to a psychic. "How did you know?"

"Honey," I told him with a condescending pat on his hand, "this isn't my first rodeo. I have 75 first cousins. Just 75 first cousins alone."

My husband is a physician, and last summer he happened to be working in the emergency department when my 90-year-old paternal grandma suddenly checked in after suffering a stroke. My parents and all my dad's siblings were out of town on a trip together and didn't have cell service. My husband called me and told me to come right away.

That afternoon we sat with my thankfully stable grandmother, fielding dozens of messages bombarding a gargantuan cousin text chain in which everyone began coordinating shifts to stay with her, cook her meals, and ensure she had constant company.

"Your family is incredible," my husband told me later that evening, shaking his head. "You are so lucky to have so many great relatives."

Just then my cousin whose wedding reception I had missed texted me a picture of our smiling grandma. "Back home in her armchair and happy," she said. "We're painting her nails tonight."

A tinge of guilt and gratitude rushed through me and a surprise tear emerged from my eye.

I think I'll make more of an effort for the next family wedding.

# The Holy Ghost Goes to Bed at Midnight

In 1993, The Church of Jesus Christ of Latter-day Saints produced a film called *Legacy*. It was about the Mormon pioneers making their way across the plains to ultimately settle Salt Lake City and open a surprising number of competing cookie and soda shops throughout the Mountain West.

This film played in a theater in downtown Salt Lake City's Joseph Smith Memorial Building for the better part of the '90s and was viewed so frequently that my friends and I could quote most of it by heart, and we did so (not with the best of intentions).

There's a scene in which the protagonist is bidding farewell to her fiancé, who is about to march off to war with the Mormon Battalion. They are silhouetted in a forest, bonneted, wind-blown and sun-kissed. "It may be in Zion when we meet again," the weepy fiancé predicts, referring to their plan to reconvene in the Salt Lake Valley and plant a water-guzzling lawn in the desert at the conclusion of his military sojourn.

The protagonist shouts in response, "If we ever meet again, it will be Zion to me."

My husband moved in 2016 to Salt Lake City, where he suddenly began learning about Mormon culture through a firehose. As a part of his education, someone, as a prank on me, began teaching him common phrases that had plagued my youth.

"If we ever meet again, it will be Zion to me," he shouted several years ago as he was leaving the house. This has since become his favorite way of saying goodbye to anyone and everyone he sees.

A couple of years ago, he added a recurring event to our shared iPhone calendar, each Sunday at 7 p.m. "Companionship Inventory," it said. A shudder ran down my spine as I read words I had blocked from my mind decades before. I spent two years as a Latter-day Saint missionary regularly engaging in an activity by the same name in which I was required to sit in awkward adolescent tension with my assigned mission companion and have a frank discussion about all the things we didn't like about each other.

"What is this?" I asked my husband about the calendar event.

"We should start setting aside a time each week to talk through our schedule and discuss ways in which we can support each other more," he said, straight-faced.

"But," I asked, "why did you call it that?"

He shrugged and changed the subject, refusing, as he always has, to reveal his sources.

"What does it mean when someone says 'the sacred ghost goes to bed at 10 o'clock?'" he asked me once.

"First of all," I began to argue with him, "it's called the 'Holy' Ghost, and it doesn't go to bed until midnight, so whoever told you that one lied to you."

I then learned how odd the title of "Holy Ghost" sounds to someone who didn't grow up hearing these words on a regular basis.

"Okay, then why does this ghost go to bed at midnight?" he asked.

"Well," I explained, "the first thing you need to understand is there's this ghost that's holy, and it hangs out, like, in good places."

"Huh," he said. "And it haunts people?"

"No," I clarified. "It follows them around, or I guess it dwells inside of them, and it whispers instructions."

He shook his head. "That sounds like a haunting. And maybe even a possession."

"No," I said. "That's not a haunting or a possession. This isn't, like, a spooky ghost. It's just a spirit that hangs around and tries to warn people about danger."

"You just gave the dictionary definition of a 'haunting,'" he responded.

I didn't feel like arguing anymore. "Well, a haunting or not, the point is our parents used to tell us it goes to bed at midnight, and that means we didn't need to be out later than that because we would be more prone to getting into trouble."

He stared at me, blinking.

I then realized that this logic, which I had always taken for granted, may not come naturally to people who are hearing it for the first time as fully formed adults.

"So, basically," he tried to summarize, "Mormon kids need to have a midnight curfew because the sacred ghost gets tired and needs to rest?"

I sighed. "No. I don't know. It's just something our parents said in the '90s because *they* were tired."

He again shrugged and walked away. An irrational rush of guilt I hadn't experienced in a decade hit me along with an implicit feeling that I had just failed as a missionary.

A few years ago, my sister asked us to stay with her kids for two days while she and her husband went out of town. My sister's family members are active Latter-day Saints, and this happened to be General Conference weekend. When I realized this, I wondered whether it somehow fell upon the irreverent family gays to make our teenage nieces and nephews watch it. We ultimately announced it was up to them and, in a surprise to no one, they opted not to spend the day tuned in to church TV.

That afternoon the kids were misbehaving in some way, prompting my agnostic husband to point at the television and shout, "If you don't straighten up, we are going to turn on the sermons!" Then he looked at me, so adorably earnest, and said, "Right?"

I paused, encouraged by the children's reaction that suggested this was an effective threat but also conflicted about using religion as a punishment.

My sister returned home late that evening and asked us for a report.

"We got the kids in bed before the Holy Ghost last night," my husband told her. "And they behaved today so we didn't have to watch that church show."

"Don't ask," I responded to her puzzled look.

As we walked to the door, my husband gave her a hug goodbye.

"We had a great time," he assured her. "Thanks for letting us come and stay with them."

"I should be thanking you," she said. "I wish we had more time to chat. We'll have to get together for dinner soon."

His face lit up and then he said it before I could stop him. "If we meet again, it will be Zion to me."

# Lemon Drops

The first time my mother-in-law visited Salt Lake City she asked me and my husband to show her around. She, a well-read history nerd and having a general fascination with religion in a purely academic sense, was particularly interested in seeing Latter-day Saint historical sites.

We took her to Temple Square, which played all the hits for her: The pin-drop presentation in the Tabernacle. The crackling overhead speaker giving "space Jesus" a robust autobiography in a strong Utah accent atop the North Visitors' Center. A sister-missionary-guided tour of Brigham Young's house(s), including a suspiciously glossed-over explanation of why he needed so many rooms. (All questions on this were forgotten after they offered us lemon drops, which disappointed my mother-in-law once she learned they were talking about hard candy and not her favorite cocktail.)

We eventually made our way over to the Conference Center. "Listen," I told my husband and his mother. "This isn't my first rodeo. If you're not careful you can easily get sucked into a 90-minute tour in this place."

I guided them into the lobby, where we were greeted by a senior sister missionary. "Please do not be offended," I said to her, "but we do not have the stamina or patience for the regular spiel. Can we please just peek in at the auditorium and then go up to the garden roof?"

Now listen. Yes, I was a guest here, and in some contexts one might argue what I requested was rude, considering that I was a guest. But I paid tithing for 30 years and got beaten up as a church missionary in Ukraine for the cause. And when you add in the number of times I cleaned a meetinghouse toilet and the one-year stint (in which I aged 10 years) when I served as Young Men president and HAD TO GO CAMPING, I figure I'm still entitled to the occasional special Deseret treatment.

I may have exchanged my temple recommend for booze and general hooliganism, but at some point I earned lifetime status at least at the lowest rewards level, and, frankly, I could cash that in on far worse things than requesting slapdash tours of religious buildings.

To her eternal credit, the senior missionary nodded at me and said "got it" in a tone like we were all on the same team here. "You guys just tell me to shut up if I start talking about something you don't want to hear. I taught middle school for my entire career. It's impossible to offend me."

We had not anticipated the tour guide might be funny, and had I thought this was a possibility, I would not have come in so hot. But there we were, 90 minutes later, on the rooftop garden watching this senior missionary deliver a five-star, one-woman show with the confidence of a veteran Broadway performer. She had jokes. Her comedic timing was enviable. She was real with us.

When my mother-in-law tepidly asked a question about the Mountain Meadows Massacre (she had just learned of this in a book), I expected apologetics and digressions. Instead, the senior missionary gave a frank and robust answer that included references and recommendations to non-church-produced historical records where we could find more information. I'm not sure whether what she did was frowned upon, and it is for this reason I am choosing to withhold her name in this column. (I ain't no snitch.)

The sun was beginning to set by this point. "Oh!" the senior missionary stopped midsentence. "This is the most perfect lighting. Do you want me to take a picture of the three of you with the Wasatch Mountains in the background?"

We accepted her offer and huddled together for a shot. "Do you want one with just the two of you now?" she asked, referring to me and my husband. "It's a very romantic atmosphere."

It was so casual, the way she said it, that I forgot the context. Here was a Latter-day Saint missionary, on the clock, offering to help my gay husband and me photographically preserve our love atop an arena where General Conference sermons regularly denounced our very relationship.

On the drive home, as the three of us excitedly discussed our new obsession with this stranger we'd likely never see again, the irony occurred to me that she had probably engaged in the most effective missionary work anyone would see that day simply by choosing to *live* a message rather than preach it.

She reminded me of so many Latter-day Saints I've known throughout my life. There are certainly plenty of the other kind, too—the ones I block on social media and hope to never accidentally move next door to.

But I've been thinking of something my dad said to me recently. I have no permission to share this, but he had no permission to bring me into the world in the first place so honestly every family secret I publicly broadcast is on him and my mother.

We were talking about religion and the history of The Church of Jesus Christ of Latter-day Saints, including some of the (ahem) more uncomfortable aspects.

"I don't think any religion is perfect, and I have a hard time with some things I learn," he told me. "But, at the end of the day, I figure if my religion is helping me be a better person and try to do good, at least there's that."

While those who use their religion to inflict harm irritate me to no end, I appreciate the other kind who are just out there hoping to succor the weak. It seems the church is packed with both types of members: the ones who use their belief as a sword against anyone who disagrees with them, and the well-meaning folks who wander between the first group, simply trying, however imperfectly, to clean up the damage.

While we may disagree on matters of faith, I'll stand in unity and friendship with the do-gooders any time, sipping my lemon drop while they suck on theirs.

# Reflections on Ukraine

In 2014, I took a trip to Ukraine to visit friends.

I had served a Latter-day Saint mission there and have returned for work or to visit many times since, but this trip proved perhaps the most memorable. It came only a few months after the heart of Kyiv was nearly burned to the ground due to political strife—the trigger that quickly launched the illegal annexation of Crimea and the invasion of Ukraine's eastern border.

The conflict happened when Ukraine's then-president, Viktor Yanukovych, rejected an economic deal with the European Union at the urging of Russia's Vladimir Putin. Many Ukrainians had seen Yanukovych as a puppet of Putin and Moscow for many years. This latest move confirmed those sentiments and sent a crowd of protesters into central Kyiv.

These sorts of peaceful protests happen in Russia from time to time. The Kremlin is quite good at stomping them out through force and arrests. It was probably for this reason Yanukovych thought it would be a good idea to send riot police after this group, who may not have made much news if he had simply ignored them.

Within a matter of two days, scores of people were killed and hundreds injured. The move ignited a fire under the demonstrators, who then spent the next several days barricading the city center with tires and furniture and pulling the cobblestones from their own ancient streets to launch at the government forces. The fighting during that bitter cold Ukrainian February led to more deaths and a substantial amount of destruction. In the end, Yanukovych fled to Russia. An emergency election was scheduled and a new government formed. (This event was well documented in the 2015 Oscar-nominated film *Winter on Fire: Ukraine's Fight for Freedom.*)

I had watched the events unfold with great sadness. Each day my go-to news sources flooded their pages with images of the streets in this city I love burned black, protesters launching Molotov cocktails in the darkness, agony all around.

When I arrived in Kyiv that May, I told the friends I was visiting I wanted to go see the city center in person. Although the fighting had ended nearly three months earlier, my Ukrainian friends discouraged me from going there.

"Too depressing," one told me.

I went anyway. To my surprise, the streets still were barricaded with tires and furniture. I was able to enter the area through an underground Metro station. It was a pleasant spring day, and as I entered the center square, I noticed how quiet it was. The absence of vehicle traffic and commercial activity had put this vibrant city to sleep.

Protesters were still camping on the streets. I don't know why they remained there, but I wondered if they had chosen to stay until the elections were held later that month. They cooked food over open fires and walked among the piles of cobblestones. Some sat watching a news broadcast on a large screen that had recently been erected on the square.

After a few minutes, I heard music. A Ukrainian women's folk group, dressed in bright traditional garb, had begun singing, and the protesters quickly gathered around to join in. Their voices and accompanying accordion echoed off the charred buildings surrounding us—the same ones that had witnessed centuries of strife. Wars. Famines. Hitler's destructive invasion in the Battle of Kyiv in 1941. Dancing in the streets when Ukraine gained its independence after the dissolution of the Soviet Union in 1991. And now, in 2014, singing.

It will forever be one of the most surreal experiences of my life. There I stood, on the cusp of my 30th birthday, among the rubble that had monopolized international news weeks earlier, in a country that felt like it was coming apart at the beginning of what would be a long, devastating war. The people there looked haggard and tired and hungry. Death had stained these streets so recently. The future seemed so precarious.

And yet, there they were, dancing and smiling and singing—together. It's always amazing to see hope spring among people who seem like they should have the least of it.

A few years later, Ukraine elected Volodymyr Zelenskyy to the presidency—a much different man and politician than his predecessor who sent riot police after peaceful protesters before fleeing his own country when things became hard. After the war escalated, when Russian troops attempted to take Kyiv in early 2022, the world witnessed a leader pushed to greatness. He was eloquent, thoughtful and fearless in the face of what many thought to be insurmountable odds.

The thing is, he's special, but I don't believe he's an anomaly. Zelenskyy is a reflection of the people who chose him. The ones who stood their ground against violent oppressors and then sang together in their sacred yet scarred streets. The ones who didn't bat an eye when I, a foreigner, approached and sang with them.

I don't believe in hero worship. I only worship my dogs. And they've earned that by being dogs.

But I'll never pass up an opportunity to be inspired by people who, amid great struggles, manage to keep being people despite it all.

# Yin and Yang: The Canine Edition

In January 2017, I rescued a dog. I like to word it that way because it makes me sound like a hero. Truthfully, I didn't do much. A friend saw a little black Cavalier poodle mix on an emotionally manipulative rescue website and sent me the link, asking if I was going to let that poor creature never find a forever home.

The next day I met an employee of the rescue organization in a Petco parking lot. I told myself I was just going to meet the puppy and then decide if I wanted to go through with it. When she handed me the 7-pound shaking dog, who smelled like horse poop, his face drenched with tears, he wrapped all four of his legs tight around my arm and stared at me so desperately I started crying.

I took him home that night, named him Duncan and gave him a gentle bath in the kitchen sink.

I don't know Duncan's history, but it seems clear he knows he comes from humble circumstances. He's highly claustrophobic, which made it impossible to crate him. Fortunately, he was easy to train. It was like he was just grateful to have a safe home and wanted to thank me by causing as little trouble as possible.

He potty-trained immediately and never chewed anything he wasn't supposed to. Before long, he started doing chores around the house. One year he helped me file our taxes. He's the kind of dog who would call 911 if one of us started choking. I love him more than I've ever loved any person. I've already informed his vet that if we ever have to put him down, I'm going to need the animal hospital to prepare enough euthanasia for an adult man as well.

This dog is such an angel that I sort of forgot all dogs are not like this. That's the reason, I guess, I thought it might be a good idea to get a second puppy.

It was November 2021, when I made one of the biggest mistakes one can make in a marriage: I bought a dog on the internet without consulting my spouse.

I blame COVID-19 for this. I had just tested positive and found myself one evening lying on the couch with a 102-degree fever. Realizing Christmas was around the corner, my fatigued brain began running through a list of gift ideas and, after a minute, I decided it might be fun to surprise my husband, Skylar, with a puppy.

For context, I had good reason to think he would generally want one. My in-laws are dog people to a degree I didn't know was possible until I met them. A few years ago, Skylar's sister informed us her aging husky mix had died during the night. I spent the rest of the day listening to my husband have sobbing phone calls with each member of his extended family over this.

I have an uncle who lives in California and had two dogs Skylar never met. One day, Skylar walked into the house with tears streaming down his cheeks. I asked what happened, expecting him to respond with news of a tragedy involving a close friend. But no.

"I just saw on social media your uncle has to put down his sweet baby, Sid."

"You don't even know this dog," I responded.

"I know," he sniffled, and his voice trailed off into high-pitched emotion. "And now I never will."

So, yes, in my COVID fog, I just assumed Skylar would think this was a grand idea simply because he loves dogs.

After a quick Google search, which I swear said "bern a doooooodle Utah pupy" (I checked later), I put down a large non-refundable deposit on a Bernese Mountain Dog poodle mix to be picked up in eight weeks and went to bed.

I awoke around 2 a.m., laughing at the bizarre dream I just had in which I purchased a dog on the internet without meeting it or checking with my husband first. A minute later, a small panic rushed through me and I reached for my phone to verify that it had, in fact, been a dream.

After I saw the confirmation email, I lay in bed for the rest of the night rehearsing over and over how I was going to tell Skylar.

That morning we took Duncan for a walk around the neighborhood, and I thought I'd gently try to feel out Skylar on this for my

Courtesy Eli McCann

own peace of mind. I thought I could maybe trick him into giving me retroactive permission.

"Do you ever worry Duncan is lonely?" I asked Skylar.

"No," he responded.

"But . . . what if we got him a brother one day," I added. "Like, maybe a Bernedoodle?"

Skylar winced. "I don't want a Bernedoodle, and this is a really bad time to get a second dog anyway," he said, noting that he was in the middle of his medical residency, and we were both working long hours.

At this point any plan to keep this a Christmas surprise was abandoned and I panic-dumped a confession onto Skylar, who instantly forgave me. (I do not deserve this man.)

Eight weeks later, we brought an absolute terror into our lives, named him Louie, and then watched him bite us, scratch us, chew through furniture, and sprint out the front door and down the street on a daily basis. At six months, he taught himself how to open gates and doors so he could no longer be easily corralled. At eight months, he was tall enough to help himself to whatever he wanted on countertops and upper cabinets.

Duncan would stand at the edge of the room, watching us try to train this monster, with a look in his eyes that said "when is he leaving?"

Whenever anyone we passed on walks commented on how cute Louie was, we'd respond, monotonically, "Thanks. Do you want him?"

It's been two and a half years since we first brought Louie home and even after expensive extensive training, he still doesn't listen to us. Just last week we had to chase him through the house to wrestle from him a loaf of bread he had stolen during the two seconds we had our backs to him.

Once we pulled the mangled carbs from his salivating mouth, he stomped to the center of the room and collapsed onto the floor in a frustrated huff. A second later, he let out a long, annoyed sigh.

I caught Skylar staring at Louie just then, a smirk on his face.

"What?" I asked him.

"I'm so glad you got COVID and bought him. I love him so much," Skylar said.

I looked at Louie, who glared back at me just as Duncan began licking his face.

"Remarkably," I said, rubbing my right arm where a new set of scratches had just formed, "so do I."

# I Didn't Ask You to Play Because You're Talented

My great aunt La Donna died in December 2023. She and I were close, and the news hit me like a freight train. But it wasn't necessarily unexpected. While La Donna was still as mentally sharp as she had always been, running her own business and leading an active social life, she was 95 and had some physical setbacks in recent years that served as a reminder to the rest of us of her mortality.

It was two years before when La Donna first called me to let me know she had begun planning her funeral and had already picked out an assignment for me.

"Your father will conduct," she said, in her usual acerbic and commanding tone that always suggested these things were not up for debate. "You will be playing the piano."

I tried to stop her right there. "La Donna," I interrupted, "my piano lessons from the early '90s were not quite the musical training I think you're anticipating."

"Nonsense," she shouted back at me before reciting the various songs she had selected for the proceedings. "I'm giving you advanced notice so you can start practicing now."

"Okay, lady," I told her. "But if you're going to make me do this, you have to live for another 15 years because that's how long I'll need to prepare."

"You don't have that long," she responded. "I could go any day now."

When my husband, Skylar, and I started objecting to this dark talk, she cut us off and said, "Oh, boys, how many 93-year-olds do you see out roaming the streets?"

When I started coming out as gay a decade ago, and subsequently began introducing Skylar to family and friends, I sometimes did so with a bit of trepidation. This was especially true with my more elderly family members, who I feared might have a harder time approaching this with grace.

Looking back, I don't know why I ever worried about telling La Donna. When I brought Skylar to see her for the first time, she embraced him, sat him down, and talked his ear off for the better part of two hours, asking him every question she could conjure.

When we said goodbye that day, she pulled me aside and took both of my hands into hers. She was a hunched, small, fiery red-headed woman with glasses half the size of her face. I looked down at her as she smiled at me. Her voice broke a little when she squeezed my hands and said, "I love you and everything you are. I love you because of who you are."

I remembered this moment when I began practicing the piano, scolding La Donna in my mind for not holding out for at least another five years, knowing that I never would have started practicing until her body was cold anyway.

Although La Donna had not been an active Latter-day Saint for most of her life, she did start attending church in her final years. The first time Skylar visited her home, he asked me why there was a picture of Jesus right next to her full bar with quite an impressive collection of international liquors. On a side table sat a picture of her with Frank Sinatra, her former employer and close personal friend.

"This woman is an enigma," I whispered. "And every fact about her is the best fact about her."

La Donna had selected four Latter-day Saint hymns for her funeral. Three were to be sung by the congregation. One was expected to be performed as a musical number by my three aunts.

I spent an hour each day, fumbling through the sheet music on my home keyboard, like an 8-year-old forced into piano lessons. To help pass the time, I began singing along as I played, although I made up my own profane lyrics for each of the songs, prompting my husband at one point to stick his head into the room and scold me. "You better stop that," he said. "You're going to get those words stuck in your head and then start laughing when you remember them while playing at the funeral."

I waved him away.

My singing aunts grabbed my arm and pulled me into a practice room the moment we arrived at the funeral home on the big day. All three of them had lost their voices recently and otherwise told me they were quite out of practice. "Why did she want us to sing?" one of them asked. "We sound terrible."

It occurred to me as we stumbled our way through one practice round that maybe La Donna had done all of this as some sort of hilarious prank.

Time had run out and my dad took to the podium to conduct and welcome my large extended family. Minutes later, I sat down at the piano and began my first of several shockingly bad performances.

Aunts, uncles, one cousin and my grandma each took turns speaking and sharing their favorite cherished and funny memories of this absolute force who had been so present in all our lives.

At the end of the service, I sat at the piano again and began playing the closing hymn, the profane lyrics I had sung during my practices running through my mind, forcing me to resist a smile. As I hit yet another wrong note, I suddenly remembered the last conversation I had with La Donna, just a couple of weeks before she died.

I had called her to check in. "Listen, honey," she said to me after we exchanged some pleasantries. "I'm de-junking my home at the moment to make it easier on everyone when I finally kick the bucket, and I found some music books I think you may want. Sheet music for the piano."

"I'll take them," I told her. "But you aren't allowed to die yet because I'm not prepared to play the piano at your funeral."

She laughed.

"I'm serious," I said. "I am really bad at the piano these days."

"Oh, honey," her shaky voice came through the phone. "I didn't ask you to play because you're talented. I asked you to play because I love you."

# Permed Mullets to the Rescue

My parents have a picture in their house of my two older sisters standing in front of a wall of sandbags. It's from the spring of 1983. It was taken on Salt Lake City's State Street, not far from the Eagle Gate arch.

This photo was a regular feature at school show-and-tell exercises throughout the 1980s and '90s in my family because of the story it told, a story I wasn't yet alive to experience (I was born the following year).

The winter of 1982–83 had brought a healthy snowpack to the Wasatch Front, one that overwhelmed our then-existing infrastructure when a precipitous runoff began flooding our state's capital the following spring.

"It seemed like everyone in the valley showed up downtown to place sandbags along State Street," my dad told me once. Maybe this is why my parents had to bring their two children, then ages 5 and 3, to the disaster site—there were no babysitters available since every shoulder in the valley was put to the wheel. Also, my fuzzy memory of being a small boy in the latter half of that decade leads me to believe there were few safety practices in the '80s, so I'm sure no one batted an eye when my hippie parents brought their toddlers to a flood like it was a tame water park for children.

In 2023 my husband, a Salt Lake City transplant, walked into the house one day after work, kicked off his snow boots, and shouted, "Should we be worried about flooding?"

It was March, and he was referring to the fact that we were on the tail end of a winter of record snowfall. I told him that although I hadn't personally experienced a winter quite that snowy before, Salt Lake City had seen some flooding in 1983 and my parents were part of a community mitigation effort, made up largely of dads and moms in acid-wash jeans and sporting bad mustaches and mullet perms. Somehow, without the use of cellphones and social media accounts to organize the assembly, they showed up to create temporary rivers down city streets to collect and ship the excess water to the Great Salt Lake.

Twenty minutes later, I found my husband slouched in front of his laptop watching news footage from that year reporting on the cleanup. As one segment ended with videos of a stripe-shirted volunteer assembly line of neighbors passing sandbags down the street, he choked up slightly and said, "I'm so proud of us for all coming together and helping."

I told him I was impressed that he had managed to take partial credit for the actions of a community he's not from during a time he wasn't even alive to witness, but he waved me away. "Oh, you know what I mean."

It was only a few weeks later when he came home again and informed me there was a need for volunteers at Sugar House Park for sandbag filling, the first of many preparation and cleanup efforts we saw throughout the state in 2023. For the next couple of months, we tracked the flooding and community efforts to redirect water and minimize damage to property and life, helping when we could.

By season's end, news outlets reported extensively on the relative success of these efforts, noting that, thanks to prudent government funding and investment, with an assist from volunteers across the state, many disasters were averted.

"I'm so proud of us," my husband told me once again before I reminded him that all we did was fill a few sandbags alongside hundreds of our neighbors.

"I don't mean you and me," he countered. "I'm proud of the whole community."

It was a reminder I receive often—that he's a better person than me, not the least of which because he implicitly manages to consider all other humans as a part of the greater "us," even in contexts where they did something before he was born.

It's nice living with a man who sees people, often in a communal sense, for their best parts. And if not that, at least for what they could be. It technically means I can get away with bad behavior more than if I had married someone critical.

I acknowledge I have to sometimes fight off the tendency, perhaps all too common among many of us, to feel cynical about these issues. To wonder if we've lost that drive to care about our neighbor, the same drive that propelled the mullets and bad mustaches in 1983 to toss their toddlers onto sandbags so they could join assembly lines of people who showed up simply because they were needed. A quick perusal of social media on any given day sure seems to support the results of my light ongoing audit on humanity.

Then again, the only reason I didn't feel my husband and I could take much credit for managing the 2023 flooding was because hundreds of our neighbors were already stuffing sandbags when we showed up, so there really wasn't much left for us to do. I'm not sure why my brain sometimes wants me to think those people are not the norm—a more accurate reflection of what most of us are, or at least want to be when we're willing to take a deep breath and try not to see strangers as enemies.

I don't know whether there will be a need for sandbags next spring. But I'm sure there won't be a shortage of volunteers if we do happen to see some flooding. And I guess I'm proud of us for that.

I'm already growing out my permed mullet in preparation.

# Late-Night Feedings

I became a dad in September 2024, just a few months after turning 40.

Most of the experience of parenthood so far has been basically what I expected: Feedings at 2 a.m. The feeling of being constantly coated in spit-up. My husband and I wandering our home day and night in an absolute zombie state, having the same conversation over and over again without realizing it. It's honestly remarkable how much of my life is now occupied with talking to another grown man about someone's pooping habits.

But there have been some unexpected side effects to becoming a dad. For example, it turns out bringing a baby into my home will cause my mother, whom I both idolize and fear, to visit us every day and say ominous and vague things like, "Oh! That's an interesting way you've chosen to do that!" Also, strangers on the internet have taken it upon themselves to send me alarming, unsolicited parenting advice that directly contradicts virtually everything our pediatrician has told us. And did you know diapers don't always work? Yes, sometimes we unswaddle the baby to learn his entire body is caked in mustard. We take turns changing him. It's the most disgusting game of Russian roulette imaginable.

My husband and I have handled the stress of trying to keep a baby alive in completely different ways. He has cleared our bank account, buying every invention that promises to make child-rearing easier. My Google search history is filled with queries such as "baby crying, dangerous?" And "baby not crying, dangerous?" And "dad crying, dangerous?"

I've always heard that it takes a village to raise a child, but I don't think I ever truly knew what that meant until a village started showing up for mine. The moment we brought our baby home, friends and family began appearing on our doorstep with casseroles like they were on a humanitarian aid mission. Had I known having a baby came with an onslaught of free food I would have done this a decade ago.

We've had nearly constant streams of visitors poking their heads into our house to drop off baby clothes and other supplies, and to peek at our son, like parades of peasants paying their respects to an infant prince. The amazing thing about these visits is how little the people stopping by care about my husband and me. I don't think a single person has made eye contact with me in nearly a month. Last week, my entire family circled the baby in our living room to worship him. I left for an hour to run errands, and when I returned, no one had noticed I was gone.

The greatest gift anyone has ever given me happened about four days after we brought him home. We were so sleep-deprived by this point that I think we were technically not considered human anymore. My younger sister called to tell me she was coming to stay the night and be on baby duty so we could catch up on sleep. I nearly started crying just at the offer and made a note to have a star named after her. I slept so well that night I saw the face of God. I was so rested the following morning I could have become fluent in Hungarian just by hearing someone speak it. I'll go the rest of my life chasing the high of that one night of glorious slumber.

We take him on walks each evening, our two dogs in tow, baby sleeping in the stroller's bassinet, totally unaware he's outside or, perhaps, even alive. We've embarked on the same walking route for many years now, often passing by the same people we've greeted for nearly a decade without ever exchanging names. I've been wondering if they've tracked my expanding family the way I've sometimes tracked theirs with joy. A decade ago, it was just me, alone and lonely, walking through the neighborhood. Eventually, it was a dog and me. Then a dog, a husband and me. Not long after that we each had a leash. And now, a stroller.

I don't mean to sound like I think I'm the main character of the world. And for all I know, no one has ever paid any attention to me on these walks. But the other day I did choke up at the thought of some stranger seeing our chaos and thinking, "I'm glad that guy doesn't look so lonely anymore." Granted, I am a

Courtesy Amanda Hall

severely sleep-deprived man with a heart bursting from the hard launch of middle-age fatherhood, so nearly anything can make me cry right now.

Like a framed image my husband asked a friend to make of our family dressed as ghosts as a surprise for me. He knows Halloween usually bums me out because I didn't have a child of my own to take trick-or-treating. "This year, you'll have all of us," he said as he handed it to me.

Last night, the baby woke up around 2 a.m. to eat. It was my turn to feed him, so I gathered him from his bed and took him to another part of the house to rock him with his bottle so as not to disturb my husband.

I don't think I'll miss late-night feedings, but I have to confess there's something about those moments that feels sacred in some way. The darkness. The coziness. The little gremlin sounds that come from his mouth as he devours three ounces of something I haven't built up the courage to taste myself, even though I am curious.

Before he came, I told people I worried I was going to be bad at all of this. I've never been very good with babies. After the feeding, I sat him on a table and set off on a groggy diaper change, and it occurred to me just then how natural this all felt—like it was something I was supposed to be doing all along, but I just didn't have the baby yet.

What a relief to find out at least some of this is intuitive. That becoming a dad feels more wonderful than odd. Yes, this really does just seem normal.

Then again, it is a pretty strange sensation to change the diaper of someone who one day may be changing mine.

# Jesus Wants Me for an Apricot Tree

Ever since we brought our new baby home, my husband and I have engaged in daily grappling over the level of this infant's general awareness. At some point, we think we have to stop swearing, but we are putting that off at least until after our son recognizes us. The logic, I guess, is that he doesn't currently know who is uttering profanity, so he's still unequipped to report any of this to my mother.

We visited my husband's family in Portland, Oregon, for the holidays. I walked into the living room on Christmas Day and found our baby sleeping on my mother-in-law's shoulder as she watched *Die Hard* with the volume turned down. "Don't you think he might be a little too young for this?" I joked as Bruce Willis walked his bare bloody feet over broken glass. "He has to see it sometime," her dismissive response came back.

The receptacle for all bad but confident parenting advice, the internet, told us before he was even born that it's important to begin to read and sing to your baby the instant he enters the world. This felt silly for at least the first month as we showed him books his eyes couldn't see and read him stories, fully understanding he doesn't know what language is. Or that he even exists. But we did it anyway because we are more scared of failure than logic.

The singing always seemed at least a little more sensible. No, he doesn't understand the lyrics, but we figured the melodies might be soothing, even to someone who hasn't yet discovered his hands.

I've experienced a strange phenomenon I absolutely did not anticipate when it comes to picking out the songs to sing. There I'll be, rocking him, and searching my mental database for appropriate material, and the next thing I know I'm almost subconsciously informing him that "Jesus wants me for a sunbeam."

Listen. I haven't been a member of a Latter-day Saint Primary for 28 years. The last time I attended church Mitt Romney was running for president, and "I'm a [Victory for Satan]" ads were plastered all over Manhattan. These songs should have been purged from my brain by now and replaced with trivia about all the trashy reality TV I've consumed in the past decade.

But no. Here I am, finding myself having to explain to my husband, who has never been religious, why someone might be dense enough to think an apricot tree is covered in popcorn balls. Or speculating about whether the pioneer children really did sing as they walked. And walked. And walked.

I don't even realize when I'm doing it. The music just pours out of me like I'm an inanimate jukebox and someone just shoved some tithing down my throat.

I did not anticipate parenthood would require me to (badly) explain to my spouse what a Lamanite is and why I was singing to our kid about it. But there I was last week, looking for a way to search, ponder and pray myself out of this habit before our son becomes old enough to start singing these tunes back at me.

Recently I found myself performing "I Belong to The Church of Jesus Christ of Latter-day Saints," so now I'm just straight up lying to this child. To make it more honest, I guess I could add a second verse about how I traded in that church membership for booze and general hooliganism, but then I'd have to find a rhyme for homosexuality, and I wouldn't even know where to start.

I suppose on some level it makes sense that Mormonism is bubbling out of my pores as I learn to become a parent. The most intimate view of child rearing I've had in my life is my own upbringing, which was framed by all the traditional Latter-day Saint milestones and everything that comes in between them. It's only natural that I'd recently catch myself starting to think about whom we should get to baptize our baby when he's 8, before remembering that, oh wait, we're not doing any of that.

Still, there's something that feels odd to this recovering Bible-thumper that there won't be some kind of religious ceremony for my second-grader down the road. Maybe there's a ceremonial antidotal event we can organize to scratch that itch when we get there—a spiritual methadone. Like, letting him get his first tattoo, maybe. (Don't worry. It will be tasteful.)

Truthfully, we don't see ourselves as a family that hates religion or distrusts anyone who values it. I was fortunate to marry a man who came in without an opinion about my childhood faith, and even though he doesn't understand most of it, whenever he sees a nice example of Christianity in practice, he's sure to give credit where credit is due.

A few years ago we were watching a film where a character made a biblical reference to the woman taken in adultery from the New Testament. My husband paused the movie to ask me for context. I explained to him this was a story of Jesus standing up for a woman who was accused and abused by a group of men who declared her a sinner. When I finished the account, my husband, with tears in his eyes, said, "Awe. Jesus seems like he was a really sweet guy. It's too bad what happened to him."

I must have laughed for five straight minutes. The way he so earnestly gave props to one of the most well-known religious figures in the world like this was a recently departed family member we were mourning.

I guess it wouldn't kill me to try to have at least a touch more of that attitude as I attempt, as a matter of course, to train myself away from reciting Primary songs. I may not plan to teach my son to take the sacrament or buy him an illustrated Book of Mormon, but I confess I wouldn't mind if, rather than take his life lessons from *Die Hard*, I saw him live the lyrics by Carol Lynn Pearson, "I'll walk with you. I'll talk with you. That's how I'll show my love for you."

After all, that was a song my loving parents sang to me, and it seems I survived it.

# Speed Bumps

I bought my home in Salt Lake City in 2014. I lived alone, which meant I could do whatever I wanted at all times, such as throw outrageous parties like teens in a '90s sitcom in which the parents went out of town for the weekend. I was so free. So alive.

Two years later, my now husband, Skylar, moved in and began asking a lot of unfair and intrusive questions like "Why do you throw your clothes on the floor instead of into the laundry basket?" or "Why don't we have a smoke detector?" or "Why do you watch so much TV?"

He went about "fixing" things for a time, bringing a level of organization to our home that is so robust it almost feels like a flaw. Did you know there is a "correct" way to load the dishwasher? Well, there is. And even though the dishes always got clean enough before he came along, I was apparently doing it the "wrong" way.

Sometimes he'll tell me I need to change how I'm doing something in the house and if I refuse, he'll accuse me of weaponized incompetence, a popular therapy phrase that describes how a spouse will purposefully perform a hated chore poorly so the other spouse will just do it next time. I'll then argue that I'm not doing the chore poorly, just differently from him, and that he is weaponizing weaponized incompetence to try to get me to do it his way. Eventually, he'll win the argument by frowning at me, which scares me into compliance.

Fortunately, a number of years ago Skylar apparently decided the house was sufficiently in order so he turned his attention to the outdoors and made everyone who lives within four blocks of us his next victims of his unsolicited project management.

It all started when we learned a child on our street had been hit by a speeding car and would have to undergo several surgeries and significant physical therapy. (The child is now doing well, in case you're worried.)

"We must do something about this," Skylar said after he told me what had happened.

I wasn't surprised he had learned this information. He's the type of person who stops to talk to strangers if they happen to be outside as he's walking by. Usually the conversation starts by Skylar complimenting the person's home or yard. Then, five minutes later, he has somehow downloaded our neighbor's life story.

For the next three years, Skylar's entire personality revolved around trying to get the city to install speed bumps on our block to slow down the ever-increasing speeding traffic and hopefully prevent this from ever happening again.

He started by going door to door, asking all the residents on our long street for their thoughts on speed bumps. The vast majority supported them. A few were apathetic. A couple of people said they would prefer some other measure.

The most significant effect of his efforts during his early neighborhood polling was that he made a lot of friends. We live in an area with many elderly residents. I work from home, and for several months I began receiving an onslaught of retirees showing up at our house during working hours looking to visit Skylar, only to appear disappointed when I explained he was at work and only I was home.

Skylar eventually moved his advocacy to community and City Council meetings, where he learned about the onerous process for submitting infrastructure project requests. This included, among other steps, a requirement that he have dozens of our neighbors sign a petition. He was already known around our area as Guy Who Collects Signatures, having done so on a number of occasions for various political causes. On a recent morning, we walked by a woman sitting on her front porch. She waved to us and Skylar shouted to her, "Don't worry! I don't have anything for you to sign today," prompting her to shout back, "Thank God."

As we walked away, he told me, "She usually refuses to sign my petitions, and she sometimes yells at me, but we've become friends anyway."

When I tell you the speed bump project became an obsession for him during this period, I mean it. Last summer, a friend came to visit. Skylar picked her up at the airport and brought her to our house. I was in the kitchen and overheard him say to our guest just as they walked through the front door, "Oh, by the way, we're about to have a baby."

The friend gasped and then responded, "Why did you just spend 20 minutes telling me about your traffic-calming measures and not that?"

"Yeah," Skylar said, "I should have led with the baby. I'm just really excited about our speed bumps."

His popularity in our neighborhood dipped last fall when, thanks to his advocacy, city crews showed up and dropped several large (very ugly) concrete barrels onto the street as a quick fix. The barrels funneled traffic into a single lane to slow down speeders. They were hit by cars almost every day. Several of our neighbors complained, each asking me some form of "Can you please get him under control?" I would respond, "I'm just happy he's so distracted with this that he forgot to force me to demolish our bathroom for a remodel I'm unqualified to perform."

The barrels eventually were removed. It was around this time that Skylar got word the speed bump petition had been approved. He responded like he had won an Oscar, listing all the people he wanted to thank, including God and his mother. (I was not mentioned in the speech.)

It still took several months for the bumps to show up, but a crew appeared and began to work on them. He watched out the window with glee, tracking their daily progress. Once the final touches were added and the workers departed, taking their orange cones with them, he wandered to the street, full of wonder, like the Munchkins exploring Munchkinland after Dorothy's house flattened the Wicked Witch of the East. He then jogged two blocks, admiring each of the four speed bumps with any neighbor who happened to be outside.

We were passing one of the speed bumps on our evening stroll recently with our two dogs and baby. Skylar was pushing the stroller as I held onto the leashes. One of our neighbors saw us

Courtesy Eli McCann

walking by, so he stepped out onto his front porch and shouted, "I've been meaning to congratulate you."

"Thank you," Skylar said. "It was a lot of work, but I've noticed the speed bumps have already slowed down the traffic, and I think they also look really nice."

The man appeared bewildered. "I was congratulating you on the new baby," he clarified.

"Oh." Skylar turned a little red. "Of course—the baby. Thank you so much. I guess I'm just excited we made our neighborhood a little safer for him."

## The Simple Hum of a People Gathered

Throughout my childhood in Utah in the 1990s, my family had a large metal bowl, usually reserved for popcorn or bland potato salad made for our gargantuan family reunions.

Everyone in the neighborhood had this same bowl. No one knew where these came from, nor could any remember when they showed up. The same thing went for our white Astro vans and those red-striped picnic blankets we summoned every summer—all staples of '90s Utah Latter-day Saint homes.

I fished out the metal bowl on Independence Day 1994, two months after I turned 10. Mom had begun making her neighborhood-famous caramel in a heavy-bottom saucepan, stirring it in professional diligence so as not to allow it to burn. My sisters and I sat on stools at the kitchen counter, watching in delight.

This was our routine, our ritual. We all had fresh sunburns from spending the morning overreacting to our underwhelming town parade that included cosplaying revolutionary soldiers in costumes assembled from a dollar store. Members of my pale Irish-descended family hadn't worn sunscreen. We were putting our futures into God's hands.

After the parade, we met our cousins, aunts and uncles at a park for a large family picnic. Dad handed us watermelon triangles he had sliced that morning. Mom poured watered-down Kool-Aid (why was it always watered down?) into our paper cups. We spent hours getting tetanus on the playground's long metal slides that were the temperature of hell itself. We ripped our skin off our knees as we carefully crawled atop the nearly serrated monkey bars that were just high enough off the compacted sand that not even the strongest among us could survive a fall. We climbed aboard one of those roundabouts with rusted metal poles as our older cousins spun us into permanent vertigo and concussions.

We never wanted to leave. Eventually, though, we made our way home so mom could start making caramel.

Mom turned from the stove, now holding the saucepan and actively stirring its contents. My oldest sister was in charge of popping so much popcorn that you could see it from space. She used the brown-and-mustard-color PopLite popcorn maker my parents had received as a wedding gift in 1976—an appliance still in active rotation among their almost exclusively vintage repertoire of kitchen amenities. I'm certain this PopLite will outlast the Giza pyramids.

There was almost no greater Pavlovian response from my childhood than hearing the sound of the first kernel ricocheting in the PopLite. It usually meant it was a Sunday night and my family, like every family in the neighborhood and perhaps country, was getting ready to gather and watch whatever made-for-TV movie or miniseries was about to premiere on ABC.

"Who the hell is calling us right now?" Dad would yell if ever the landline rang during these sacred hours.

There was no way to pause the program. No way to rewind. We'd let the call go to an answering machine—a device from the future we had incorporated into our home only a few years before. We had all gathered around Dad as he nervously recorded the outgoing message, like he was King George VI delivering his landmark radio address at the cusp of World War II.

Mom began slowly pouring the steaming caramel over the hot popcorn in the metal bowl, using a large wooden spoon in her other hand to begin mixing it. Minutes later, she had formed 4-inch balls, set to cool on a warped baking sheet (another immortal, although embattled, wedding gift). They would be hard as diamonds by night's end.

Just as the sun set, we pulled our beach chairs to the driveway and the red-striped picnic blanket to the front lawn. Dad began opening the cheap variety pack of wispy fireworks he had purchased from the pop-up stand in the Ream's parking lot at the end of the street. Every father in the neighborhood had bought this same pack—well, besides that one rumored family a few blocks away that had smuggled in military-grade weapons, probably from some cartel.

The families up and down the street started making their way toward our house, carrying their own beach chairs and red-striped blankets, deciding we might as well consolidate the firework display, especially considering the likelihood that half our supplies were statistically duds. Our house was the gathering place, probably because of the large metal bowl of now-cooled popcorn balls that had made its way to the festivities.

This happened every year, but it always felt spontaneous.

The kids ran amok, occasionally scolded by the army of neighborhood dads who, for the price of $19.99 each, were channeling their most militant instincts to re-create the Revolutionary War on our suburban street.

"You're going to burn your eyebrows off," one of them shouted as an undeterred 6-year-old hopped over one of those lit blue spinners that probably had a name none of us knew.

The teens gathered on the picnic blankets, whispering about whatever it was teens found interesting back then.

A 10-year-old was chipping his teeth on his fifth popcorn ball.

One of the moms could be heard to say, "You know, we have this same metal bowl at home."

Eventually, the display dwindled, and the parents circled their beach chairs to engage in grown-up conversation while the children instigated a game of tag in the dark. Echoes of pops and cracks could still be heard. Off in the distance, we caught obscured glimpses of a professional firework show at some park miles away.

All these years later, I still think there's no better sound than the general background noise of neighbors being neighbors—the simple hum of a people gathered, sans devices and distractions, satisfied by company and the shared community that company builds.

Social media, some politicians and many other of the loudest voices would have us sometimes believe these scenes are no more—that division and exclusion are the norm.

But I think most people are the type to sit on beach chairs and laugh together. The type to gladly ruin their dental work on someone else's homemade caramel popcorn. The type to gather without invitation, almost instinctively, before packing it all up and heading home, looking forward to next year when they get to do it all again.

# Glossary

**Baptism:** Latter-day Saint baptisms typically take place in church meetinghouses where a baptismal font allows for full immersion under water (a quick dunk). Children in Latter-day Saint families are usually baptized at age 8.

**Beehive State:** Utah's nickname, a reference to the Mormon pioneers' originally naming Utah "Deseret," a Book of Mormon word meaning "honeybee."

**Bishop:** Each ward (congregation) is presided over by a bishop, a man in the neighborhood who is asked to volunteer to serve in that role for several years at a time.

**Branch:** When there are not enough Latter-day Saints in a particular geographic area to make up a ward (usually a few hundred congregants), a "branch" is instead formed, often drawing fewer than 50 people to Sunday services.

**BYU Honor Code Office:** An office at Brigham Young University tasked with enforcing the provisions of the Honor Code, through which BYU students vow to obey a set of rules, such as a commitment to avoid pre-marital hanky-panky.

**Companion:** Young Latter-day Saint missionaries are assigned other young Latter-day Saint missionaries to be their "companions," staying together 24/7 for several weeks or months at a time. Mission companionships are periodically changed to allow missionaries some variety over the course of their 18-month or two-year mission.

**Companionship Inventory:** A dreaded weekly practice where missionaries are required to sit down with their companion and discuss openly whether the missionaries are annoying one another.

**Deseret:** A word derived from the Book of Mormon meaning "honeybee," often used to describe Latter-day Saint populations and their proclivity toward productivity and community, similar to the little buzzing creatures.

**Elders Quorum:** A group of adult Latter-day Saint men in a congregation make up a group called the "elders quorum."

***Ensign*:** For many decades, The Church of Jesus Christ of Latter-day Saints produced a monthly magazine called the *Ensign*. Faith-promoting stories printed in the magazine were often the source material for a religious sermon or lesson.

**Family Home Evening:** Latter-day Saint leaders have encouraged church members to designate Monday evenings for family time to play games, teach religious lessons, and fight with each other.

**Family Proclamation:** In 1995, Latter-day Saint leaders penned a document detailing the faith's beliefs around the concept of family; over the years, the proclamation's unequivocal defining of marriage inclusive only of straight couples has caused much fervor and debate.

**Fast and Testimony Meeting:** On the first Sunday of each month, sacrament meeting in Latter-day Saint congregations is opened up for congregants to take the mic as they wish and share their feelings about their faith.

**General Conference:** Every six months, in the spring and autumn, the church conducts a series of broadcasted meetings from Salt Lake City where church leaders share religious sermons. Most Latter-day Saints watch the meeting from their homes or at their local church meetinghouse.

**Home Teaching:** For many years, The Church of Jesus Christ of Latter-day Saints conducted a program called "home teaching," where the men of each congregation were assigned in pairs to visit a few families once a month and make awkward small talk for 30 minutes before sharing a religious quote and leaving as quickly as possible.

**Jell-O Belt:** A play on the term "Bible Belt" to describe a string of southern states, someone decided to refer to Utah and parts of its surrounding states, where one can find a critical mass of Latter-day Saints, the "Jell-O Belt," a wink at the culture's love of the sweet treat (sometimes served with shredded carrots).

**Lamanite:** The Book of Mormon discusses the history of several groups of people living in ancient America, including the "Lamanites."

**Mission:** The term throughout this exceptional book refers to the formal program in which teens just out of high school and retired couples don little black nametags and live somewhere in the world for up to two years, looking for new recruits to join The Church of Jesus Christ of Latter-day Saints.

**Missionary Training Center:** Latter-day Saint missionaries are sent to a campus for a crash course on how to be a missionary, including language training where applicable, for several weeks at the beginning of their service. The largest of these campuses is in Provo, Utah.

**Mountain Meadows Massacre:** In one of the ugliest and most shameful chapters in Latter-day Saint history, a group of Latter-day Saints slaughtered more than 100 weary travelers in 1857 as the travelers attempted to peacefully pass through Utah.

**Nauvoo, Illinois, and Kirtland, Ohio:** Two historic towns where the Mormon pioneers dwelt for a time on their way west to present-day Salt Lake City.

**Pioneer Day:** A Utah state holiday on July 24, celebrating the day in 1847 when Mormon pioneers entered the Salt Lake Valley and began building a community. Non-Latter-day Saints in Utah often celebrate the holiday as "Pie and Beer Day," electing to forego the covered wagons and cosplaying pioneers, opting instead for pizza, pie, and alcoholic beverages.

**Priesthood Session:** General Conference includes one session for priesthood holders, only—male Latter-day Saints, ages 12 and up.

**Primary:** Children under 12 make up a group in Latter-day Saint congregations called "Primary." Each Sunday they gather to sing and hear religious messages.

**Sacrament Meeting:** Latter-day Saint congregants gather on Sundays for a one-hour meeting to take the sacrament, sing hymns, and hear sermons from other congregants. There is always at least one baby crying.

***Saturday's Warrior*****:** A musical from the 1970s, committed to film a decade later, wherein parents of a teen boy are concerned about his friends' influence on him, which has led him into so much hooliganism that he now cares about the environment and over-population of the planet.

**Space Jesus:** My nickname for a statue of Jesus Christ that for many years sat under a dome on Temple Square in Salt Lake City, which dome was painted to look like it was dotted with stars and planets. This dome has since been razed as a part of a massive renovation of Temple Square.

**Stake:** A collection of Latter-day Saint wards (congregations) in a geographic area are grouped together to form a stake, which is led by a stake president and his counselors.

**Tabernacle Pin-drop Presentation:** While giving tours of the Salt Lake Tabernacle (built in the 1860s) on Temple Square, missionaries drop a pin onto the wooden pulpit at the front of the large building, which makes a sound that can be heard all the way at the back, demonstrating the superb acoustics and pioneer ingenuity.

**Tithing Settlement:** An awkward annual meeting where one must sit across a desk from their neighbor who has been asked to volunteer as bishop (leader of the ward) and discuss how much money the congregant paid to the church that year.

**Trek:** Latter-day Saint teens are often dragged into the wilderness during the hottest week of the summer to cosplay as Mormon pioneers making their way across the plains. To my knowledge, no one has ever participated in this activity willingly.

**Victory for Satan:** Latter-day Saint church president Russell Nelson made it a pet issue when ascending to his leadership role to weed out the use of the word "Mormon," stating that acceptance of that word amounted to a "victory for Satan."

**Ward:** Latter-day Saint congregations are called "wards." I don't know why. I just work here.

**Word of Wisdom:** Church founder Joseph Smith penned a series of health guidelines, which Latter-day Saints have followed to varying degrees ever since, including prohibitions on alcohol, coffee, and tea.

**Young Men:** Latter-day Saint boys, ages 11 to 18, make up a congregation's "Young Men" group, meeting together on Sundays and one evening a week.

**Zion:** The Mormon pioneers of the nineteenth century trekked west for a land they called "Zion," a longed-for utopia, which they found in present-day Utah. Note, please pronounce this word correctly if you ever visit Utah (rhymes with lion).

# About the Author

Eli McCann is a lawyer, writer, and podcaster. His monthly humor column for *The Salt Lake Tribune* explores cultural and religious ideas, usually through his experiences living as a gay man in Utah. Since 2016, McCann has produced and cohosted the storytelling podcast and live show, *Strangerville*. His work has been featured in publications around the world, including *The Washington Post*, *Newsweek*, *HuffPost*, *BBC*, and others. His writing and other creative projects can be found at his website, itjustgetsstranger.com.